the healing anxiety workbook

a guide to calm worry and intrusive thoughts at the root

SHERYL LISA FINN

SOUNDS TRUE INNER WORKBOOKS

Sounds True
Boulder, CO

© 2025 Sheryl Lisa Finn

Sounds True is a trademark of Sounds True Inc.

All rights reserved. No part of this book may be used or reproduced in any manner without written permission from the author and publisher.

No AI Training: Without in any way limiting the author's and publisher's exclusive rights under copyright, any use of this publication to "train" generative artificial intelligence (AI) technologies to generate text is expressly prohibited. The author reserves all rights to license uses of this work for generative AI training and development of machine learning language models.

This book is not intended as a substitute for the medical recommendations of physicians, mental health professionals, or other health-care providers. Rather, it is intended to offer information to help the reader cooperate with physicians, mental health professionals, and health-care providers in a mutual quest for optimal well-being. We advise readers to carefully review and understand the ideas presented and to seek the advice of a qualified professional before attempting to use them.

Published 2025

Cover design by Rachael Murray
Jacket design by Charli Barnes
Book design by Meredith Jarrett

Tree of Life diagram inspired by the ten Sephirot, the primary mystical symbol of the Kabbalah.

Printed in the United States of America

BK07167

ISBN: 978-1-64963-367-5
Ebook ISBN: 978-1-64963-368-2

contents

Introduction *1*
    Foundational Exercise: Who Sits at the Head of Your Table? *11*
        Attributes of a Loving Wise Self/Inner Parent *12*
        Indicators of an Absent or Quiet Wise Self/Inner Parent *13*
        Finding Your Wise Self/Inner Parent *14*
        Growing Your Wise Self/Inner Parent *16*
    Connection Inventory *20*

part one   connected to self

    Connecting to Body *31*
        In the Garden Visualization *33*
        From Shame to Awe *34*
        Creating from the Body *36*
        Busy Hands, Calm Mind *38*
        Move Your Body and Let It Be Fun *41*
        Making a Plan to Move Your Body *43*
    Connecting to Heart *47*
        Emotionally Connected *48*
        Compassion for Your Younger Self *52*
        Beliefs about Pain *54*
        Responding to Beliefs about Pain *58*
        Tonglen Practice to Breathe in Pain, Breathe out Comfort *60*
        Embrace Joy *62*
        Everyday Joy *64*

Connecting to Mind 67
- Identifying Core Stories 68
- Writing to Release Core Stories 73
- Map and Visualization to Lay Down Core Stories 76
- Engage Your Mind 81
- Take a Class or Workshop 84
- Stop Ruminating by Reading a Poem 87
- One Small Text 89

Connecting to Soul 93
- Connection and Disconnection from Our Phones 94
- Screen Sabbath 98
- The Pause in Your Day 101
- Practice the Pause with Me 104
- Pause and Poetry 106
- Visualization to Cleanse and Release 108
- Dreamwork 110
- Dream Mandala 114

part two   connected to others

Connecting to Friends, Family, Partner, Animals 119
- Non-Human Friends 120
- A Friendship Tree 122
- Partner Gratitude 124
- Family Stories 126

Connecting to Local Community 129
- The Connectivity of Neighbors 130
- Community Connections 133
- Widening the Circle 136

Connecting to Purpose 139
- What's Your Soulprint? 140
- The Myth of a Calling 144
- The Gifts That Are Longing to Be Seen 146
- We Cannot Save the Whole World 150

part three connected to the unseen

- Connecting to Ancestors *155*
  - Family Stories and History *156*
  - Family Recipes *158*
  - Ask an Ancestor to Take Your Worry *160*
  - Offer Gratitude to Ancestors *162*
- Connecting to Creativity and Spirituality *167*
  - Start and End Your Day with Song *168*
  - Replace Intrusive Thoughts with a Song *170*
  - Return to Your Dance *172*
  - Connect to Gratitude *174*
  - On Repeat: From Worry to Mantra *176*
  - Bake Bread *178*
- Connecting to Nature *183*
  - Be in Nature *184*
  - Befriend a Tree *186*
  - Every Stone Tells a Story *188*
  - Embraced by Night *191*

Conclusion *195*

Acknowledgments *197*
Recommended Resources *199*
About the Author *201*

introduction

anxiety is one of the most distressing symptoms of our times. When I tell people that I work in the realm of anxiety, they invariably respond with some version of, "Well, you must be very busy." Anxiety is, indeed, pervasive, and it's on the rise: there has been a 50 percent increase in anxiety disorders over the last three decades and three hundred million people suffer from anxiety globally. Yet, this number only accounts for those who seek a diagnosis. The reality is the actual number of people who struggle with anxiety on a daily basis and never seek support is significantly higher.

In short, humans are anxious. And we have some good reasons to be. Anxiety is a healthy response to actual danger, and, while many of us are living in safer times in our day-to-day lives than ever before, we're also aware of highly anxiety-provoking threats, from the climate crisis to gun violence to war. On a personal level there's also more expectation on us to "succeed," and our support systems have radically decreased, which increases the pressure on everyone. Furthermore, while technology connects us in some ways, it also disconnects us, creating more isolation and less community. These are all factors that contribute to the modern incarnation of anxiety.

Anxiety is, in a nutshell, a lack of safety. Sometimes the sense of danger originates from an external source, like the threat or reality of war, insufficient resources, or school shootings, and sometimes it originates internally from a hypervigilant scanner that is constantly searching for danger. When there is real-and-present danger, anxiety serves us well; it can spur us to study harder for an upcoming test, and it can alert us to the presence of an immediate threat. But anxiety has a habit of snow-balling into pervasive worry and intrusive thoughts, even when there isn't an immediate or obvious threat. This is when anxiety stops serving us and instead becomes a different sort of messenger designed to alert us to internal places that need our attention.

Let me pause here to say that healing anxiety isn't entirely an internal job. If you can't pay your bills and you live in a country that doesn't take care of its citizens, this is inherently anxiety-provoking, and doing your inner work isn't going to change the outer situation. There are many broken systems in our world that, if fixed, would radically reduce anxiety. For anxiety, alongside the sense of being unsafe, is also the sense of not being taken care of. If you trusted that there were communities and structures in place to take care of your basic needs, these aspects of anxiety would naturally abate. When I talk about anxiety as a lack of safety in this book, I'm referring to inner safety. I want to be clear at the outset that by referring to inner safety I am by no means invalidating or simplifying the very real external systems that need a radical overhaul so that all people feel taken care of, have their basic needs met, and feel safe.

Anxiety that isn't centered around our basic human needs often shifts into the territory of worry and intrusive thoughts. While many therapeutic approaches seek to reduce symptoms by changing our thoughts and behavior, my work is informed by the depth psychological tradition, which aims to not only shift our thoughts and behavior but also heal our symptoms at the root. Symptom reduction is essential, and for many people it's an effective approach to working with anxiety. Yet, for others, once the intensity of the symptoms has been reduced, they're left with what the symptoms were covering over, which can be anything from unhealed trauma to grief to the pervasive sense of disconnection that permeates our modern lives.

The Power of Connection

In my previous book, *The Wisdom of Anxiety*, I addressed many of the underlying root causes of anxiety, focusing specifically on anxiety as a messenger alerting us to inner places that are off-kilter in our four realms of self: physical, emotional, cognitive, and spiritual. This workbook addresses these elements as well but through the lens of connection. For among the many roots causes of anxiety, one of the most pervasive is our disconnection in three primary directions: from self, others, and the unseen realms. When we reverse engineer this root cause, we can begin to repair the ruptures by asking: what creates connection? When we're connected in all sphere—when we belong to ourselves, to others, and to the unseen realm (nature, ancestors, creativity)—we feel securely attached, a fullness of being emerges, anxiety is edged out, and we trust in the goodness of life and our place in the order of things. Life no longer feels quite so fragmented and tenuous, and we're able to move forward in each moment with more presence, purpose, trust, and joy.

> When we feel bone-and-soul safe—the type of safety that cannot be taken away—intrusive thoughts, obsessions, anxiety, worry, and compulsions quiet down, even when life feels uncertain.

The basic equation is: Attachment = Safety.

When you are healthfully attached in all directions, meaning you feel connected, you feel filled up and safe, and anxiety is less likely to seep in. On the other hand, when there are breaks in attachment, anxiety is more likely to trickle into the gaps. Again, anxiety is, at the core, a lack of safety, so when we create safety, *which is also deep trust,* in all directions, anxiety quiets down.

When we're connected, we're tapped into the flow of the world. This warm energy of goodness and light enters our soul and possibly our bloodstream, filling us with positive energy. For those of you who are more scientifically minded, we now have evidence that regular practices like meditation and prayer flood our brains, and then our bodies, with many positive neurotransmitters, most significantly serotonin. When serotonin increases, anxiety and depression decrease. This is good medicine. When we engage enough with the actions and mindsets that fill us, we replace the negative habits of anxiety and rumination with the positive actions that lead to more well-being. This workbook offers tangible ways to help you find your own pathways back to reconnection so you can feel more securely attached and, thus, safer.

Intention

When we're approaching a new project or pathway of healing, intention is key. When you're feeling anxious, the default response is to try to get rid of or fix the anxiety. All beings are wired to avoid pain or discomfort and seek pleasure or comfort, and humans are no different. However, when we seek to banish any parts of ourselves they tend to grow louder and more powerful, for all parts of us need to be seen and heard, and that includes our pain. When we try to banish anxiety, it finds its way back in another form.

My work with anxiety has primarily focused on listening closely to anxiety's emissaries of symptoms—intrusive thoughts, worry, obsessions, compulsions, insomnia—to address what is needed at the root. This workbook, while addressing the root cause of disconnection, seeks to widen the container of who we are so that anxiety plays a smaller part in our lives. We aren't seeking to get rid of anxiety so much as growing the goodness of the spheres of connection, which will overpower the anxiety. As we become more spacious through the process of re-connection, anxiety is absorbed. Salt in a cup of water is undrinkable, but the same amount of salt in a lake is unnoticeable. If anxiety is the salt, let's become the lake.

Just as love is stronger than fear, connection is stronger than anxiety.

Do not underestimate the power of connection to dissolve anxiety. Connection fuels our hearts and our world, and when it's lacking, things fall apart and anxiety ramps up in response. Just as trees communicate through a complex underground mycelium network—named by German forester Peter Wohlleben as the "woodwide web"—we, too, are connected in ways that are often unseen and forgotten. It's time to remember.

Connection is safety.

Connection is trust.

When you are held in trust, you feel safe.

Since anxiety is fundamentally the sense of feeling unsafe, connection is the remedy.

The Tree of Life

The foundational connective image for this workbook is the Tree of Life. From Celtic, Norse, Mesopotamian, Zulu, and Mayan mythology to the Kabbalah and the Book of Genesis, the Tree of Life has been an archetypal symbol of connection, groundedness, family and ancestry, and personal growth for thousands of years.

The ancient resonance of the Tree of Life indicates that humans have long known what scientists are now proving: trees live in a complex network of connection. As forest ecologist Suzanne Simard wrote in her book, *Finding the Mother Tree: Discovering the Wisdom of the Forest*, "I discovered that [the trees] are in a web of interdependence, linked by a system of underground channels, where they perceive and connect and relate with an ancient intricacy and wisdom that can no longer be denied."

We, too, live in a complex network of connection. Connection is key to our well-being. Connection to our root systems, both literally and metaphorically, brings us into our true places of belonging. "As above so below" is a common phrase in Jungian and mystical worlds: when we are connected to the world above us (the sky, the spiritual realm, clear ideas, creativity, ancestors) and to the world below (the unconscious realm of dreams, our bodies, the ground beneath our feet, human connection), there's a natural flow of energy that creates inner harmony. And when we're in harmony and equanimity—when we trust in our places of belonging—anxiety is edged out.

Belonging is more powerful than anxiety.

As you can see in the Tree of Life image, I've divided the tree into three sections to represent the three elements of connection we'll be working with in this book: the trunk is our connection to **Self** (body, mind, heart, soul), the right branches are our connection to **others** (friends, family, partner, animals, local community, purpose), and the left branches are our connection to the **unseen** realm (creativity, ancestors, nature). When we're connected in all three realms and all ten spheres, we feel attached, safe, and grounded, and anxiety naturally recedes.

Connection is more powerful than anxiety.

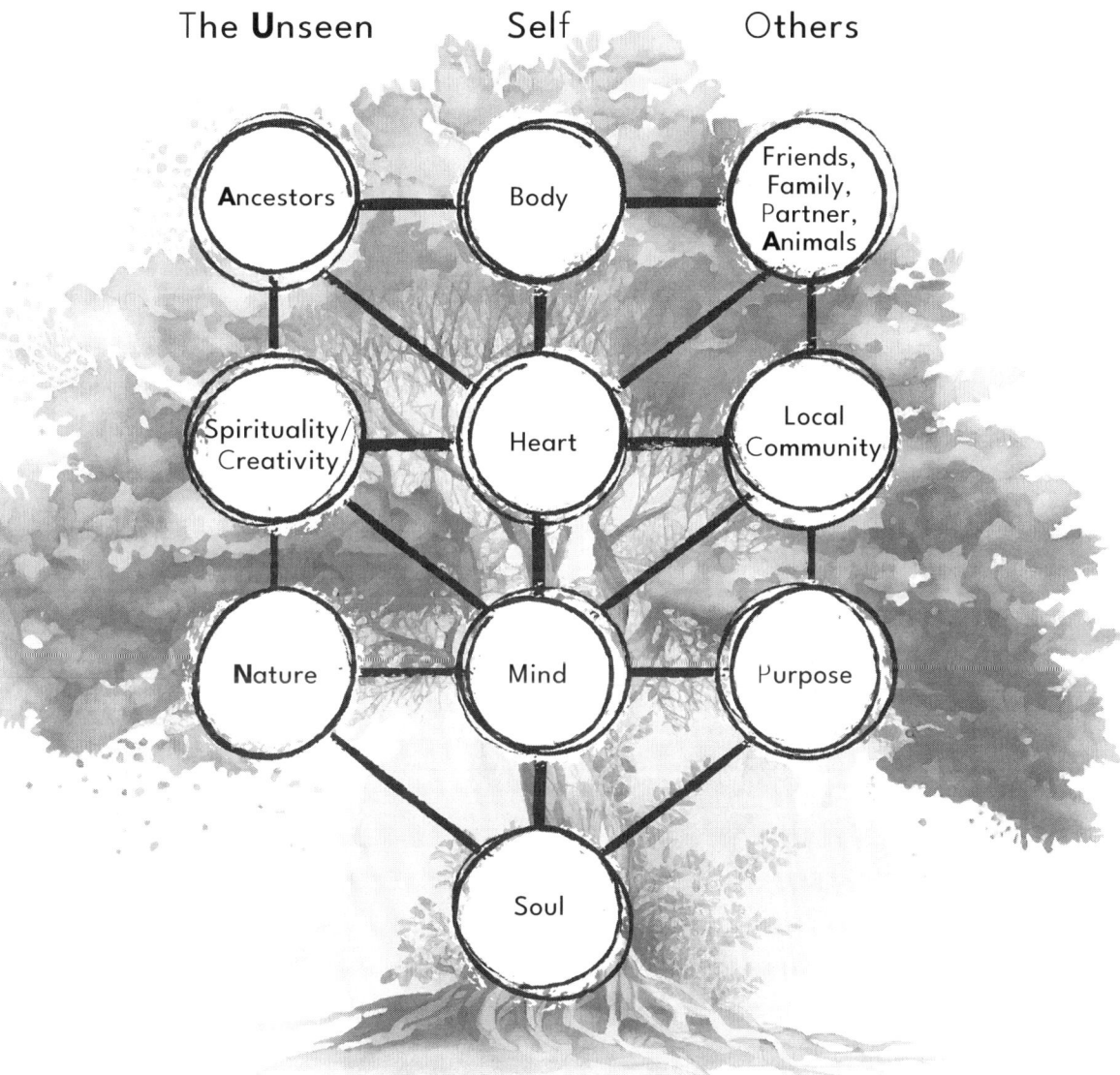

The Tree of Life

The Power of Action

This workbook, like all workbooks, is action-based. You can read and listen and learn for years, but unless you take actions that create more well-being, you will remain stuck. While accurate information is important and often transformative, it's the compassionate actions we take on our own behalf that create long-lasting, deep-rooted, sustainable change.

In order to take action, we must be able to access our Inner Parent/Loving Adult/Wise Self (these are interchangeable terms; use whichever one resonates with you). This is the part of us that is willing to do some work in order to create change. We all have an inner teen that would much rather sit around all day on our phones instead of taking loving action. While rest is essential, if inaction becomes our primary default mode, we will remain stuck and anxiety will continue to take root and fester. This is why we'll be starting with the Foundational Action of connecting with your Wise Self/Inner Parent, which you'll find at the end of the introduction. This is an important exercise, especially if you struggle with resistance.

Playing with this Workbook

Although this is a *work*book, I encourage you to approach it with a sense of *play*. While there is no doubt that anxiety can be debilitating and excruciating, when we focus on the connective elements of the Tree of Life, we begin to notice some nourishment and life-affirming qualities entering through our roots, branches, and leaves. As I often say, whatever we water will grow; if we water anxiety, we will feel more anxious, as anxiety is fundamentally an experience of being disconnected. But if we shift the focus of our attention onto places of connection, we re-enter the stream of vitality that is waiting to receive us. We are meant to be connected. We are meant to feel fully alive. We often think of inner work as hard work, but I encourage you to approach this book from a different place inside of you.

There is, of course, a time and a place to do the hard work of healing trauma and excavating the most painful places of our stories. That's what therapy is for because when we address our deepest layers of pain, which often take root in childhood, it can be very helpful to have a wise, loving, and skilled therapist facilitating the process. Once we've addressed those layers of inner healing, this book can help fill in the gaps, the ruptures of attachment that are a result of growing up in a culture that, overall, teaches us to disconnect We all have gateways back to our places of belonging. This workbook will help you find your personal pathways back to connection.

This book is meant to be a place of free creative expression. Get out your markers, crayons, watercolors, scissors, glue, and tape! Let it be fun. As I've been teaching for years, sensitivity is at the core of anxiety. When this core of sensitivity isn't honored, it often morphs into anxiety. But when sensitivity receives the attunement it needs, it channels into spirituality and creativity. This work(play)book is an opportunity to re-parent yourself by pouring attention into the ten spheres in the Tree of Life in loving ways so you can re-attach to yourself, others, and the invisible realm. Remember the equation: Attachment = Safety. When you feel safe, anxiety diminishes.

Filled with your reflections, meaningful documents, and possibly some poetry and art, this can also serve as a keepsake that you can refer to when you're feeling off-kilter. As a document of connection, it will be a reminder of all of the ways you are already connected. Sometimes all we need is a simple reminder of the places of connection—one poem or family recipe—to tap us back in.

Gold Star Practices

Throughout the book, certain exercises are labeled as Gold Star Practices, which are exercises that touch on multiple spheres of the Tree of Life at once. In the Western world, we tend to parse and divide ourselves and our lives into disparate sections: the body separate from the mind, the mind separate from the soul. In school we divide up subjects, as if history has nothing to do with psychology and math stands on an island of its own. For organizational purposes, it's convenient to divide into parts—just as I've done for this book—but in reality nothing is as separate as we think. While many of the exercises in this book touch on multiple spheres, the Gold Star Practices do so with particular potency. If you only incorporate a few exercises into your life, I recommend choosing the Gold Stars.

foundational exercise: who sits at the head of your table?

In order to attend to the ten spheres and find wellness and equanimity, we need to have a loving, competent, and clear loving adult at the helm of our psyche. Just as kids feel safe when there's an attuned adult sitting at the head of the metaphoric dinner table, our inner characters—which might include Anxiety, Judgment, Fear, Jealousy, Critic, Taskmaster, Good Child—feel safe when there's a loving, clear, attuned Parent/Loving Adult/Wise Self at the head of the table of psyche.

While I'm primarily using the term "Inner Parent," please use any other terms that feel more aligned for you. For some people, especially those who had a difficult relationship with their parents, the term "Inner Parent" could feel triggering. Many of my clients prefer the term "Wise Self" when referring to the part of us that is steady, regulated, clear, and loving. Similarly, if you didn't have a loving parent growing up, or your parent was loving but didn't know how to model nourishing self-care, you might have some confusion about what this part actually looks like. The following should help clarify.

Attributes of a Loving Wise Self/Inner Parent

As you read through the following, make a note of how your Wise Self is already showing up in your life.

- Just as a loving outer parent listens to and honors a child's needs yet pushes them past their comfort zone when necessary, so a loving Inner Parent brings compassion and intense curiosity to our inner world while making sure that we don't fall into the realm of indulgent pain. When you have a loving parent at the head of the table, you can feel your difficult feelings—sadness, jealousy, disappointment, anger, frustration, loneliness, boredom—without being swallowed by them.

- Just as a loving outer parent carves out time to drop down into the present moment and connect eye-to-eye and heart-to-heart with their child without distraction, so the Inner Parent recognizes how essential it is to create long pauses in the otherwise run-on sentence of our increasingly fast and busy days so they can listen with full presence to what's needed. This means that phones are turned off or placed in another room. It means that we hush the voices—the work, the calls, the emails, the bills—that pull us away from presence. We cannot feel safe, loved, or worthy if the parents in our lives—both outer and inner—forget how to listen.

- In addition to listening and holding, the loving, wise parent is the part of ourselves that sets boundaries and limits. It's the part that says "yes" to this (yes, I'm going to exercise now even though I don't "feel" like it) and "no" to that (no, I'm not going to drink alcohol tonight because I know it will cause me to wake up feeling anxious tomorrow). It's the part that can make decisions and trust those decisions.

Indicators of an **Ab**sent or Quiet Wise Self/ Inner Parent

The following questions and statements can indicate that you're struggling to invite a solid, loving wise parent to sit at the head.

 As you read through them, check which ones resonate the most.

It's okay if you check all of them! The more you can identify the fears and beliefs that prevent you from showing up with full responsibility, the more you can gently challenge them. Self-compassion is key every step of the way.

- ○ What if I start to feel my sadness and pain and I fall into a deep depression?

- ○ What if the sadness takes over and I can't get out of it?

- ○ What if I grow and I learn that I have to leave my loving, wonderful partner?

- ○ If I have a thought, it must be true. If I have a feeling, I have to act on it.

Finding Your Wise Self/Inner Parent

Naming the other characters in your psyche that vie for the position at the head of the table can help you identify and grow your inner parent.

> **At the table, your Inner Parent is the "Loving, Wise Self" at the head. Fill in the rest of the seats with the supporting cast members of your inner world, the parts that make a lot of noise: Resistance, Fear, Loneliness, Judgment, Arrogance, etc.**

When you engage with any of these parts, please do so with the resolute commitment to keep your Wise Self at the head of the conversation. We make room for Judgment, but we don't let it run the show. We explore the churning waters of Fear while the Loving Adult holds the tether on solid shore.

Loving,
Wise Self

Growing Your Wise Self/Inner Parent

Many people believe they don't have an Inner Parent at all, yet when I ask them if they're able to offer sound advice and a compassionate ear to friends or family members, the answer is unanimously yes. If you can listen to others, you can listen to yourself. If you can access a voice of wisdom and clarity for others, you can find that same place inside yourself. But because you likely learned to externalize your sense of self and rely on others for reassurance and guidance from an early age, this muscle has grown weak.

Now it's time to strengthen it so you can sit at the head of your table without fear of the parade of thoughts, feelings, characters, and decisions that define a human life. For it's not the thoughts or feelings that create the problems; it's how we respond. It's the Wise Self that chooses how to respond, and it's that one micro-moment that makes the difference between becoming caught in the undertow of anxiety or finding freedom.

→ How strong does your Inner Parent feel today?

Take a moment to consider something you're struggling with. How might your Inner Parent/Wise Self respond to someone else experiencing this same struggle? Offer these insights to yourself and write them below. This will serve as evidence that even though you might not believe you have an Inner Parent/Wise Self, you are wiser than you think!

Imagine yourself as a young child feeling sad, lonely, frustrated, or disappointed. Now imagine that the most loving version of yourself enters the room and sits down next to young you. What happens next? How would you have wanted a safe and loving adult to respond to your hard feelings when you were young? See yourself doing that now and write or draw what you see.

connection inventory

The following inventory will help you start to identify your personal areas of connection and disconnection in the ten realms of the Tree of Life. What we can name, focus on, and bring our attention to, we can heal. We'll be delving more deeply into each of the ten spheres throughout the book, but this initial exercise will give you a baseline understanding of each area of connection. If you check a lot of boxes, that's an area of strong connection for you. If you don't check many boxes, that's likely a sphere that needs more attention.

It's okay if there are a lot of areas of disconnection; there are for most people. It's okay if you're not clear on your purpose or calling; many people struggle in this area. It's okay if you only have a couple of friends or you don't have a best friend or "friend group"; most people don't. The intention here is to name the spheres of disconnect and slowly, over time, start to fill them in. That's what this workbook will help you do.

Check all **b**oxes that apply, then **f**ill in the **b**lanks **w**ith your **ow**n ideas.

Relationship to Self

→ **What makes** you feel **b**alanced, alive, and connected in your **b**ody?

- ○ Getting good sleep
- ○ Moving my body
    - ○ treadmill/elliptical
    - ○ martial arts
    - ○ swimming
    - ○ hiking
    - ○ walking
    - ○ running
    - ○ weights
    - ○ sit-ups
    - ○ bike riding
    - ○ yoga
    - ○ adaptive yoga
    - ○ pool yoga
    - ○ dance
    - ○ chair stretching
    - ○ swaying along to music
    - ○ gentle stretching in bed
    - ○ _____
    - ○ _____
- ○ Eating food that supports my health
- ○ Staying hydrated

➡️ **What makes you feel centered and full in your heart (the realm of emotions and relationships)?**

- ○ Laughing
- ○ Crying when I'm sad
- ○ Spending time in nature
- ○ Spending time with friends
- ○ Feeling connected to my partner
- ○ Swimming
- ○ Dancing
- ○ Letting myself feel the full range of my feelings (including sadness, frustration, disappointment, jealousy, loneliness, boredom) without trying to fix or change them
- ○ Handling my anger in healthy ways
- ○ Attending to my shame with compassion
- ○ Expressing my feelings vulnerably
- ○ Identifying my needs and expressing them responsibly
- ○ Trusting myself and others
- ○ Connecting to gratitude
- ○ Loving myself by learning how to be a loving parent to my inner child
- ○ _____
- ○ _____

What makes your mind feel engaged, nourished, and calm?

- ○ Reading or listening to books I'm interested in
- ○ Learning new things
- ○ Going to museums
- ○ Traveling to new places or exploring new spots near home
- ○ Having interesting conversations
- ○ Learning new languages
- ○ Memorizing poems
- ○ Doing puzzles
- ○ Playing cards
- ○ Playing games
- ○ Meditating
- ○ Gardening
- ○ _____
- ○ _____

What helps your soul feel nourished and filled up?

- ○ Talking about dreams
- ○ Connecting to gratitude
- ○ Blessing the beauty of the natural world
- ○ Conducting meaningful rituals

- ⃝ Listening to music
- ⃝ Being in nature
- ⃝ Traveling
- ⃝ Praying
- ⃝ Learning about spirituality
- ⃝ Playing music
- ⃝ Writing poetry
- ⃝ Knitting/sewing
- ⃝ Working with my hands
- ⃝ _____
- ⃝ _____

Relationship to Others

🌿 My family, friends, and animal connections are (**write down their names**):

- ⃝ Partner _____
- ⃝ Children _____
- ⃝ Friends _____
- ⃝ Parents _____
- ⃝ Siblings _____
- ⃝ Cousins _____

- ○ In-laws _____
- ○ Pets _____

What helps you feel connected to local community?

- ○ Talking with neighbors
- ○ Going to the local coffee shop, bakery, library, grocery store, etc.
- ○ Volunteering
- ○ Connecting with parents and children through school

What helps you feel passion (interests) and purpose (think about what lit you up as a kid)?

- ○ Reading
- ○ Gardening
- ○ Helping others
- ○ Engineering
- ○ Art
- ○ Reading poetry
- ○ Spirituality
- ○ Nature
- ○ History
- ○ _____

- ○ Playing music
- ○ Writing poetry
- ○ Science
- ○ Psychology
- ○ Writing
- ○ Listening to others
- ○ Religion
- ○ Politics
- ○ _____
- ○ _____

Relationship to the Invisible Realm

→ What helps you feel connected to your creativity and spirituality?

- ○ Expressing kindness
- ○ Drawing
- ○ Listening to music
- ○ Singing
- ○ Offering gratitude
- ○ Arranging flowers
- ○ Chanting
- ○ _____
- ○ Giving to charity
- ○ Playing music
- ○ Dancing
- ○ Blessing nature
- ○ Making sculptures
- ○ Praying
- ○ Meditating
- ○ _____

What helps you feel connected to your ancestors?

- ○ Telling family stories
- ○ Making recipes from my culture
- ○ Reading stories from my lineage
- ○ Looking at family photos
- ○ Celebrating holidays from my lineage
- ○ Listening to music from my culture
- ○ Enacting family traditions
- ○ Traveling to my homeland
- ○ Talking to departed ancestors
- ○ _____
- ○ _____

➤ What helps you feel connected to nature?

- ◯ Beach
- ◯ Boats
- ◯ Sky
- ◯ Creeks
- ◯ Lakes
- ◯ Forests
- ◯ Mountains
- ◯ Snow
- ◯ Rain
- ◯ Mist/fog
- ◯ High places with expansive views
- ◯ Sunshine
- ◯ Seasons
- ◯ _____
- ◯ _____

Now that you've completed the inventory, you have a broad overview of your spheres of connection and those areas in which you're more disconnected. This will help you start to amplify the spheres of stronger connection and pour the light of your attention onto areas that feel less full. When you're consistently attached in all ten spheres, anxiety is edged out and you start to experience more fullness, well-being, and joy.

The Self is the trunk of the Tree of Life and is comprised of our connection to our body, our heart, our mind, and our soul. This is our central column, the core from which the right and left branches of the tree extend. Because many of us were raised in ways that disconnected us from the innate wisdom of our sense of Self, learning how to fill in these gaps is essential when it comes to healing anxiety at the root.

part one
connected to self

connecting to body

Our body is our sanctuary, an awesome miracle that allows us to function on this planet. We begin here because it encapsulates three of the four realms of self: physical, emotional, and soul. The body also houses the mind, but we'll focus on the connection between our thoughts and anxiety later in the workbook. Also, since anxiety is primarily a headspace, the more we can drop down and connect with our bodies, the less anxious we tend to feel.

Physical: Our body is our grounding cord. It's how we move through the world, how we physically function, how we eat, sleep, breathe, ingest and eliminate, move, hug, make love, and procreate. Our bodies are messengers. It's through our symptoms that we know ourselves, our needs, and what's off-kilter.

Emotional: Our body is the vessel for our emotional realm, as it communicates through sensation, and it's through sensation that we come into contact with our feelings.

Soul: Our body is the conduit for soul and the transmitter of soul's expressions. It's through our bodies that we can receive the beauty of music, poetry, nature, dance. Our bodies are like the radio antenna that allow us to receive Spirit's transmission.

in the garden visualization

I invite you to connect with your body by following the QR code below and listening to the visualization "In the Garden." When you're done, come back to this page and draw, write, or color any images, phrases, or insights that dropped into your body while you were doing the exercise. An audio recording and the text of this visualization are available at:

soundstrue.com/the-healing-anxiety-workbook-bonus

or scan me!

Connected to Self

from shame to awe

We should learn early in life to revere our bodies every day for the miracles that they are, and yet many of us are taught the opposite. Many children learn very early in their lives that their bodies are a source of shame and should be hidden. It's time we reclaim what is rightfully ours: the exquisite miracle of these bodies.

Shame is a disconnector. When you're mired in shame, you lose touch with your body, sometimes even forgetting that you live in one. This shame-induced disconnect leads to anxiety. Focusing on awe can help reverse this shame.

Biologically speaking, the fact that our bodies even exist and function and know how to pump blood and digest and eliminate and breathe on their own is miraculous.

The fact that a female body knows how to grow a placenta and gestate a baby and create milk to nourish the baby is *awe*some.

The fact that an adult human is made up of around 7,000,000,000,000,000,000,000,000,000 (7 octillion) atoms is mind-blowing.

Every atom in your body is billions of years old. Hydrogen, the most common element in the universe and a major feature of your body, was produced in the Big Bang 13.7 billion years ago. Heavier atoms, such as carbon and oxygen, were forged in stars between seven billion and twelve billion years ago and blasted across space when the stars exploded. This means that the components of your body are truly ancient: you are stardust.

Yes, you are stardust.

Focus on cultivating awe for your body as a way to reduce shame and increase connection.

From the moment you wake up until you get into bed, I invite you to notice twenty miraculous ways that your body functions.

Notice your breath. Notice your digestion. Notice your senses. Keep this book with you throughout the day so you can write them below:

1. *I am amazed that I can breathe.*
2.
3.
4.
5.
6.
7.
8.
9.
10.
11.
12.
13.
14.
15.
16.
17.
18.
19.
20.

creating from the body

Through writing or drawing, let's explore the ways you disconnect from your body and become curious about pathways to reconnect. Let the wisdom come from your body. You might draw a picture or write a poem felt from your body. Set a timer for ten minutes as you consider the following prompts:

These are the ways that I judge, malign, ignore, and/or shame my body.

If my body were fully loved, this is what it would tell me, look like, say, or do.

busy hands, calm mind

If you have a mind that is highly active with chatter and rumination, try working with your hands. There is ample evidence to show that working with our hands reduces anxiety.

There is a direct connection between our hands and minds, and for most of history, humans have naturally activated this connection. But with our increasingly sedentary lifestyles, we tend to ignore the work we used to do with our hands.

As Kelly Lambert wrote in the book *Lifting Depression: A Neuroscientist's Hands-On Approach to Activating Your Brain's Healing Power*:

> "What revs up the crucial effort-driven rewards circuit—the fuel, if you will—is generated by doing certain types of physical activities, especially ones that involve your hands. It's important that these actions produce a result you can see, feel, and touch, such as knitting a sweater or tending a garden. Such actions and their associated thoughts, plans, and ultimate results change the physiology and chemical makeup of the effort-driven rewards circuit, activating it in an energized way. I call the emotional sense of well-being that results effort-driven rewards."

Here are some ways to use your hands.

→ **Check any that call to you—either ones that you already do or things you would like to try—then commit to doing it in the next twenty-four hours.**

Thinking about working with your hands is not the same as actually *working* with your hands! Let your body lead.

- ○ Crocheting
- ○ Knitting
- ○ Cross-stitching
- ○ Gardening
- ○ Pottery
- ○ Painting
- ○ Drawing
- ○ Doing puzzles
- ○ Kneading dough (see the Bake Bread exercise in the Creativity section for more on this action)
- ○ Flower arranging
- ○ Fidget toys
- ○ Making beaded jewelry
- ○ Playing guitar
- ○ Playing piano
- ○ Creating prayer bundles with sage, roses, and crystals
- ○ _____
- ○ _____

What do you notice about your anxiety when you engage your hands. Does it diminish? Does it increase? If you notice an uptick, that's normal as you get accustomed to shifting out of the head space of anxiety and dropping into your body. I encourage you to stay with the activity until you start to notice more calm.

move your body and let it be fun

One of anxiety's messages is: move your body. Movement is connection, and sometimes the simple act of movement is enough to sweep anxiety through.

Moving our bodies is literally medicine, in that it releases endorphins as well as the neurotransmitter norepinephrine, both of which improve mental clarity, self-esteem, sleep quality, and our ability to handle stress. The Anxiety & Depression Association of America says that "a brisk walk or other simple activity can deliver several hours of relief, similar to taking an aspirin for a headache." And a study from the Harvard Medical School Special Health Report showed that exercise can be as effective as antidepressant medication, and its effects last longer.

Many people struggle to find a form of movement they can commit to consistently. They also become overwhelmed by the belief that exercise has to come in a certain package or look a certain way. We need to move our bodies, but that doesn't mean we need to join the gym and suffer through an aerobics class five times a week (unless that's your thing). In fact, according to the Anxiety & Depression Association of America, ". . . a 10-minute walk may be just as good as a 45-minute workout."

Check any of the following body movements you enjoy:

- ○ Raking leaves
- ○ Shoveling snow
- ○ Gardening
- ○ Cleaning
- ○ Sweeping
- ○ Walking
- ○ Dancing
- ○ Running
- ○ Lifting weights
- ○ Swimming
- ○ Stretching
- ○ Yoga

making a plan to move your body

Human bodies are designed to move throughout the day, yet many of us have become increasingly sedentary. For most of human history, people moved their bodies as part of their daily lives. Exercise wasn't something separate from the rhythm of life any more than eating. In other words, people didn't intentionally exercise so much as the way they lived their lives—hunting, cooking, washing, walking down to the water—kept their bodies healthy.

Because life today is largely sedentary, we now have to make a point of moving our bodies on a daily basis. What we've gained in modern conveniences we've lost in terms of an effortless relationship to physical health. If you live a more sedentary life, one of anxiety's messages is to get up and move.

So . . . now it's time to get up and move! This is where resistance often shows up, as there are countless ways to avoid movement. What's streaming today on my screen? A thousand things! What's happening on social media? The infinite scroll! As much as you know how helpful it is to move your body in a loving way, this is an area where we must access the loving parent who says, "I know you don't feel like it, but we're going to do it anyway."

↗ **One of the most effective ways to work with resistance is to name it.**

How does resistance show up for you? In other words, what are the specific ways you avoid moving your body? (I've given a couple of hints on the previous page.)

_____
_____
_____
_____
_____
_____
_____
_____
_____

At the end of the day, the only way to address resistance is to take the counteraction. So, now it's time to make a place for it today. Can you move your body right now? Come on, you can do it! I encourage you to embrace any kind of movement that's possible for you, whether that's standing up and walking around for a few minutes or putting on music and dancing. If that's not possible, can you make a plan to move your body sometime today?

It can be very helpful to have a schedule for when you're going to move your body, especially if you lead a very full life.

🌿 **In the space below, write down the days and times you are most likely to move and what kind of movement it will be.**

For example, I try to take a yoga class every Sunday at 10 am, so I would add that to my calendar below.

Monday	
Tuesday	
Wednesday	
Thursday	
Friday	
Saturday	
Sunday	

connecting to heart

One of anxiety's most urgent messages is to attend to the sphere of the heart. As young people, we often learn to cut off or shut down emotionally because we don't have a safe adult to hold us when we're feeling big feelings. Feelings then register as "unsafe," and anxiety, often in the form of worry or intrusive thoughts, steps in to rescue us from the overwhelm and vulnerability of our feelings.

As Michael Singer writes in *The Untethered Soul*, "Every time you resist and close, you are building up the pain inside. It's like damming up a stream. You are then forced to use the psyche to create a layer of distance between you who experiences the pain and the pain itself. *That is what all the noise is inside your mind: an attempt to avoid the stored pain.*" Conversely, when we're emotionally connected, anxiety falls away as we no longer need it to serve as a protector against the stored pain.

emotionally connected

What does it meant to be emotionally connected?

My simple definition is this:

To attend to your feelings with compassion without indulging them or identifying with them.

Let's break this down:

To attend to your feelings means you notice when a feeling arises and you make room for it. You name it, you breathe into it, and you make a space for it at the table of psyche. The opposite of attending to feelings would be to push them away, squash them, deny them, or avoid them. This is how we've been taught, both in families and culturally, to handle feelings.

With compassion means that when difficult feelings arise, we don't judge them or shame them.

Without indulging them or identifying with them means that you feel the feelings without getting lost in them or hinging your identity onto them. When we indulge or identify, we take on a mindset that says, *My sadness is who I am, and it's all of who I am.* In this way, feelings can take over and prevent us from living our lives. They can also take over in our relationships, which means they take up all the space.

Here's a simple yet powerful exercise to help you attend to your feelings:

 Designate pause points through the day to stop whatever you're doing, close your eyes, and tune into your heart.

Simply ask yourself, *What am I feeling right now?* You might be feeling tired, overwhelmed, or anxious. You might be feeling excited, joyful, or content. You might be feeling numb or empty. There is no right or wrong way to feel; they're simply your feelings and all they need is your loving, nonjudgmental attention—the kind of attention you might have craved in your early years from a loving adult.

Let's try it now. Pause and tune into your heart. What are you feeling?

What compassion can you extend to these feelings?

What can you say to yourself to remind yourself that you don't have to get lost in these feelings and they are not you?

_____

What other times today will you pause?

_____

You can set a reminder on your phone so you remember to check in. Eventually, with enough consistent practice, this will become second nature.

compassion for your younger self

This exercise invites us to deepen our connection to our Loving Inner Parent/Wise Self to meet our pain with lovingkindness.

 **Find a photo of yourself as a young person and paste it here.**

If you can't find a photo, a drawing will suffice, but it's worth the effort to find a photo if you can.

Look at the photo, holding the intention you wrote on page 50, about how you would like to attend to difficult feelings, in your heart. This will help you remember that our emotional self is also our young self, and you can more easily practice emotional connection.

How do you feel when you look at the photo of young you?

_____

_____

_____

Calling on the highest part of you, what words of compassion and soothing can you offer your younger self?

_____

_____

_____

beliefs about pain

As we gently move into the emotional realm, it can be helpful to identify the beliefs you're carrying about pain. Since what we believe determines much of how we act and feel, when we can name the beliefs that block us from feeling the range of pain to joy, we can start to soften them and make shifts.

> **The more we open our hearts to the full spectrum of the emotional human experience, the quieter our anxiety becomes.**

It's almost impossible to grow up in our feelings-averse culture and not develop a host of faulty and fear-based beliefs about pain, all of which can be simmered down to one belief: *It's not safe to feel my feelings.*

**Review the following and check all that apply.
Feel free to add your own if any come to mind.**

These are the messages about feelings that I received growing up (either overtly or implicitly):

- ○ "You're too sensitive."
- ○ "Get over it."
- ○ "Children should be seen and not heard."
- ○ "What's wrong with you?"
- ○ "If you don't stop crying, I'll give you something to cry about."
- ○ "Feelings are weak."
- ○ "Buck up."
- ○ _____
- ○ _____

These are the beliefs that I still carry about feelings:

- ○ My feelings are too much.
- ○ Feelings are weak.
- ○ Feelings are embarrassing.
- ○ Feelings are for sissies.
- ○ I'm not supposed to cry.
- ○ I don't have time to feel.
- ○ Feelings are too vulnerable.
- ○ It's not safe to feel.
- ○ People who can avoid their feelings are strong.
- ○ If I feel my feelings, I will be judged.
- ○ I'm too sensitive.
- ○ If I feel my feelings, I will get overwhelmed, lose control, go crazy, or die.
- ○ If I feel my feelings, I will never stop feeling them.
- ○ If I feel my feelings, I'll fall into a depression and won't be able to get out.
- ○ If I feel my feelings, I will be abandoned.
- ○ I should control my feelings.

- ○ Feelings are inconvenient.
- ○ My life is fine the way it is. Why should I learn to feel my feelings?
- ○ I should fix my feelings.
- ○ Feelings are not okay.
- ○ Pain lives in the past, and that's where it should remain.
- ○ That was a long time ago, and there's no sense in dredging it all back up.
- ○ I'm too frozen. I'm a lost cause. I feel numb, and I'll never be able to thaw out.
- ○ I had a hard experience but good parents, so to grieve would be denying all that *has* gone well.

- ○ _____
- ○ _____

For now, just naming the beliefs can help you begin to heal them. The next exercise will take you more deeply into the healing process.

responding to beliefs about pain

Now, we're going to harness the Wise Self/Loving Parent and respond to your beliefs about pain. These beliefs are coming from your child self, and even though you may consciously know that they're not true, they're still running the show. When you can respond to defensive beliefs from a wise and loving place inside of you, you will start to rewire the neural pathways that are informed by the belief that it's not safe to feel your feelings, which will allow your feelings to thaw out, thus reducing anxiety.

If you're telling yourself the story that you're a lost cause and you will never safely feel your feelings, please rewrite and reframe that. Look for places where your heart opens: with animals, the underdog archetype, anywhere. You're here because you're anxious, which means you're also highly sensitive and empathic. Your heart works just fine. Through this workbook, you're building trust that you can handle your emotions.

↗ **Write down your top five beliefs about pain and respond to each one from your Wise Self.**

If you're not sure what to say, imagine how you would respond to a friend who was sharing these beliefs with you. This is an opportunity to practice accessing the part of you that is connected to compassion and wisdom.

1. _____

2. _____

3. _____

4. _____

5. _____

tonglen practice to breathe in pain, breathe out comfort

It can be helpful to have a simple practice that helps us rewire our habitual response to push away pain. One of the most powerful practices I know for helping us move toward pain instead of away from it is the Buddhist practice of Tonglen.

The practice is very simple: breathe in what we normally think of as "not wanted" and breathe out what's wanted. As the Buddhist nun Pema Chödrön says, "When you do Tonglen *on the spot,* simply breathe in and breathe out, taking in pain and sending out spaciousness and relief." When we practice this over time, we retrain the mind to accept and even welcome pain.

Tonglen can be done as a formal practice, but it's more commonly known as an "on-the-spot" practice, which means that whenever you notice a moment of sadness, fear, loneliness, disappointment, frustration, anger, jealousy, excitement, or joy throughout the day, I encourage you to pause, notice the feeling, name it as best you can, then breathe into it and breathe out the opposite.

For example, I breathe in grief and breathe out comfort for every animal on the side of the road whose life has been taken by human encroachment. *I'm sorry. I love you.* I breathe in pain every time I hear the siren of an ambulance or fire engine, and I breathe out that whoever is hurt finds peace and comfort. *May you be surrounded by love.* When I give money to people without homes, I also breathe in their pain and loneliness and breathe out love. *May you find shelter.*

When I hear of tragedies—terrorist attacks or natural disasters—the first thing I do is open my heart to the heartbreak. Other, more tangible actions, will likely follow from allowing our hearts to break open.

I invite you to pause now and notice what you're feeling in this moment. Breathe into it, then breathe out the opposite—or the remedy.

This might sound like, *I breathe in emptiness. I breathe out fullness.* Or *I breathe in sadness. I breathe out comfort.* Practicing this now will help you call on it throughout the day and week. The more you practice, the more you reverse your default habit of pushing away pain, which is one of the root causes of anxiety.

Make a list of all the times in a day or throughout a week when you notice pain, grief, disappointment, or loneliness in your heart, and take note of what it's like to practice Tonglen instead of pushing the painful feelings away.

embrace joy

Joy is one of our greatest connectors, and, consequently, one of the most powerful ways to widen the lake that absorbs anxiety.

**When we are fully in joy,
it's very hard to feel anxious.**

↪ Write about a time when you were fully joyous.

As you write, notice what it feels like in your body to reinhabit joy through the portal of memory. If you have a photo that encapsulates this memory, tape or glue it here, or you can draw a reminder.

everyday joy

Even though we know how wonderfully connecting and life-affirming it is to step into joy, many people are more afraid of joy than they are of pain. Why would this be?

Joy is vulnerable, for underneath it lives the fear of loss. The thinking goes like this: *If I embrace joy and acknowledge goodness and blessings, I'm tempting fate and something bad will happen. It's not safe to feel joy.*

But it's actually the opposite that's true: when we widen our capacity for joy, we increase our blessings.

So, let's be brave, "tempt fate," and practice embracing joy. Yes, embracing joy is a practice because it asks us to rewire from our conditioned learning that has taught us to be tentative about joy. Just like we must practice feeling painful feelings, we must practice feeling positive feelings. This is how we continue to widen the heart's capacity to feel fully, and, in doing so, we connect more deeply and edge out anxiety.

Either throughout the day or before bed, chart any moments of joy you experience, including very small joys or pleasures.

I recommend opening a page in the Notes app of your phone and noting when you feel joy. Then you can come back here and fill it in. Joy begets more joy. The more you notice, the more you teach your heart and mind that it's safe to feel joy.

Anxiety withers in the presence of joy.

1.

2.

3.

4.

5.

6. _____

7. _____

8. _____

9. _____

10. _____

    I also encourage you to use Tonglen to practice feeling joy. Every time you feel joyful, pause for a moment, breathe into the joy, and breathe out . . . more joy! As you practice joy, you teach your mind that it is, in fact, safe to feel joy. The safer you feel, the less anxious you feel.

connecting to mind

When our minds are engaged, clear, and nourished, anxiety recedes. If we're not mindful, it's easier for us to fill our minds with content that doesn't nourish us, which often leaves us feeling bored, unsatisfied, and more susceptible to anxiety. Furthermore, we often have a backlog of core stories that can play into our minds' tendency to ruminate. By identifying our core stories, we can begin to unhook from them when they arise and shift toward tending to our minds with care. It's an emptying out of what is not serving us so we can fill up and connect with what does. Remember: the more connected we are, the less room there is for anxiety to seep into the cracks. An engaged, clear mind is a nourished mind, and a nourished mind has no need for anxiety.

identifying core stories

Our core stories are a complex web of beliefs, patterns, and feelings formed around certain themes that derive from our early relationships with parents, siblings, teachers, and peers. One painful incident can birth a story, but it usually takes a repeated pattern of interaction or messages to ingrain the experience as a story.

Not all of your stories come from your personal history; many are inherited stories that were passed down through the bloodline of your ancestors, and some come from culture and religion. You may have inherited your mother's shame or your father's fear. You may have absorbed harmful messages about yourself from mainstream or social media. In one way or another, very few of your stories are directly yours, as whatever you believe about yourself likely originated in one of your parents, and their parents before them and before them, or from siblings, peers, teachers, religion, or media. The stories are handed down like genetics until they land in the most sensitive child or the one most ready to heal. That person is likely you.

In order to shift or heal our core stories, we first have to find out what they are. Here is a checklist of the common core stories.

↗ **Note any that stand out for you.**

Broad Stories about Worthiness (also known as shame stories):

- ○ I'm not attractive.
- ○ There's something fundamentally wrong with me.
- ○ Nobody appreciates me; it's like I'm invisible.
- ○ The world is against me.
- ○ My body isn't okay the way it is (I'm too fat, too skinny, wrong in some way).
- ○ I'm broken.
- ○ I'm wrong.
- ○ I'm too defensive.
- ○ There's something wrong with my sexuality.
- ○ I don't deserve goodness.
- ○ My self-worth hinges on my performance and achievement. If I "fail," I'm unworthy.
- ○ If I don't achieve, I am worthless.
- ○ _____
- ○ _____

Specific Shame Stories:

- ○ I had a sibling who was the golden child, and I always felt less than them (less attractive, less intelligent, less social, less loved).
- ○ I was put in the "slow" or "dumb" class at school.
- ○ There was one particular teacher who singled me out and shamed me.
- ○ I was bullied at school.
- ○ I was teased by my friends.
- ○ I was a late bloomer, and the people I desired didn't notice me.
- ○ I was always insecure about my body or some part of my body.
- ○ I never knew how to dress.
- ○ I grew up poor, and everyone around me had more than I did.
- ○ My parents argued a lot. (When parents argue a lot, children tend to feel insecure.)
- ○ My parents divorced, and on some level, I always felt like it was my fault.
- ○ I was told that I was too sensitive. Nobody knew how to honor and hold my feelings. I've always felt like I was too much in some way.
- ○ I was told that I was weak.
- ○ My parents would get irritated if I didn't understand something quickly enough.
- ○ _____
- ○ _____

Stories about Safety:

- ○ The world isn't safe.
- ○ I'm not safe.
- ○ There isn't enough for everyone.
- ○ My worry prevents bad things from happening. If I stop worrying, bad things will happen.
- ○ _____
- ○ _____

Stories about Emotions—Mine and Others:

- ○ My emotions are too much (too big, too loud, too dramatic).
- ○ I'm too sensitive.
- ○ If someone is angry, they might leave and never come back. Therefore I have to chase after them to make sure they don't leave.
- ○ I am responsible for others' feelings; for example, if someone is angry, it's my fault.
- ○ I can't handle anger, either mine or others'.
- ○ I can't handle big feelings. If I let myself feel them, they will overwhelm me.
- ○ _____
- ○ _____

Stories about Needs:

- ○ It's not safe to have needs.

- ○ There's no point in having needs since nobody will meet them anyway. I'll just handle it on my own.

- ○ If I ask for what I need, I'll be disappointed and dropped.

- ○ My needs don't matter. I exist to serve other people.

- ○ _____

- ○ _____

writing to release core stories

Now that you've identified some of your core stories, let's prepare to release them. What we can name, we can release, and now is the time to name what you are ready to let go of. Of course, some stories will be harder to release than others, especially if you've been carrying them for decades. Be patient with yourself and know that with enough time, intention, and practice, the stories will soften and eventually release.

 As you respond to the following prompts, don't censor or edit yourself.

You don't need to write in complete sentences. It doesn't have to make sense; just trust what arises. You don't even have to use words. Draw a picture. Write a poem. Color. Leave the perfectionist at the door. I recommend setting a timer for ten minutes so you can give yourself enough time to get deep but also know you'll be able to stop soon. If you finish before the ten minutes are up, sit quietly and breathe, get up and walk around, then listen to see if there's more, and perhaps continue.

Connected to Self

Which of the core stories that you identified earlier are you ready to release?

I am ready to release . . .

If I could release this, I imagine I would feel . . .

map and visualization to lay down core stories

We're going to take it deeper now as we visualize and embody our core stories, then utilize an element of nature and our imagination to lay them down. This is a Gold Star Practice, as it connects us to our body, mind, nature, and ancestors.

 First, refer **back** to the **I**dentifying Core Stories **q**uestionnaire and **w**rite your top si**x** core stories in the visual **m**ap.

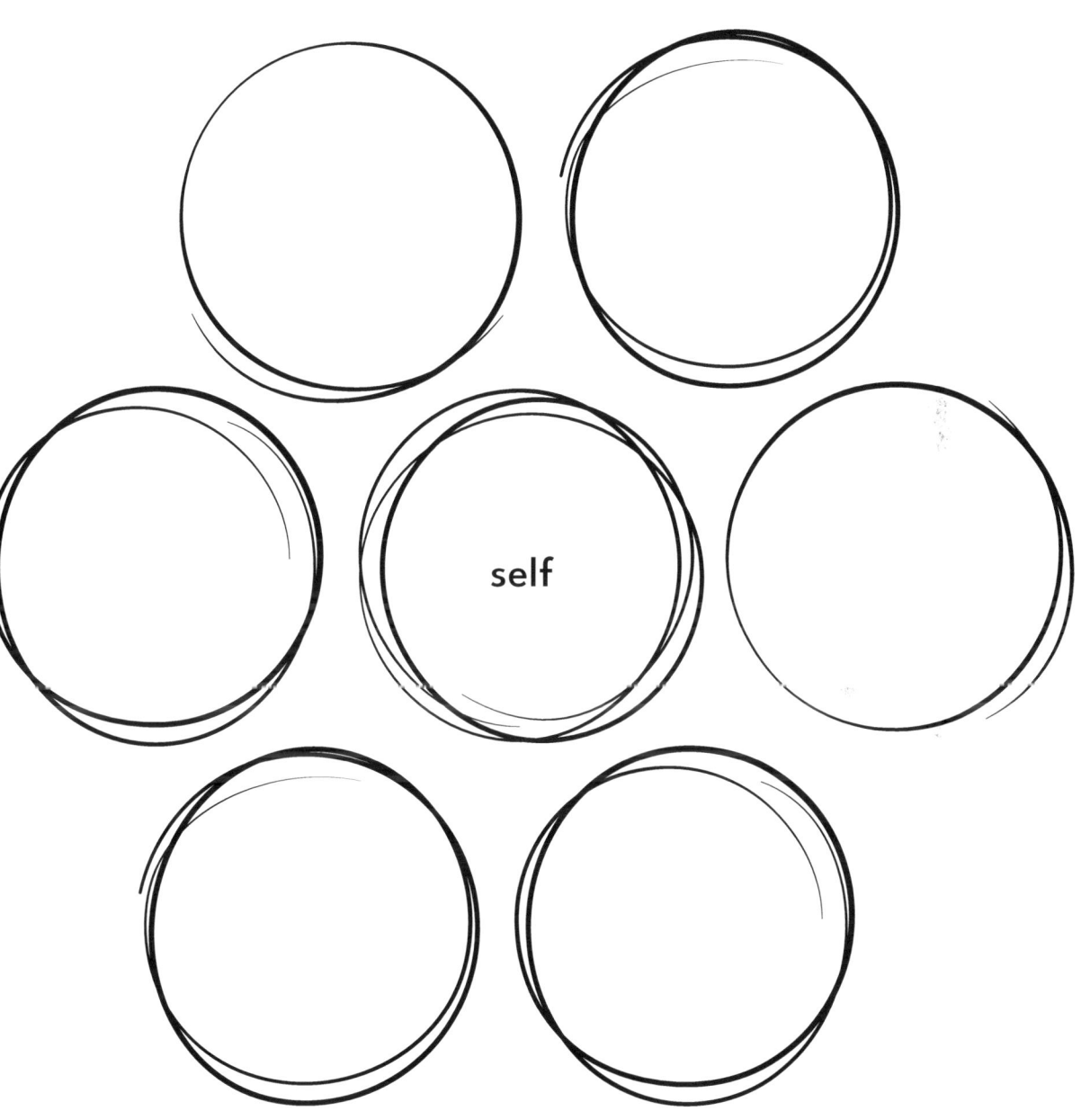

Next, practice this visualization to release core stories. An audio recording of this visualization is available at:

soundstrue.com/the-healing-anxiety-workbook-bonus

or scan me!

Now close your eyes if that's comfortable for you, and imagine that you are sitting in front of a beautiful tree. Perhaps it's a tree that you see every day, like one that sits in your yard or on the sidewalk in front of your house. Maybe it's a tree from your childhood. Imagine that this tree wants to participate in your healing and is now asking for one core story or pattern.

You see yourself approaching this tree, sitting next to the tree, talking to the tree about what is most wrapped around your heart or soul, the beliefs or patterns that are ready to be released. Allow what needs the most attention to rise up, and see yourself laying it at the base of this tree. You may even see yourself leaving the entire visual map at the tree.

Now imagine that an ancestor or a loving imaginal ally/animal is here to support your healing. You may have to suspend disbelief as you choose to trust that this tree and ally can help relieve you of at least one story, if not more. Don't overthink. Trust whatever and whoever arrives in support of your healing.

What core story did you work with?

_____
_____
_____

What ally supported you?

_____
_____
_____

How did you feel during the visualization, and how do you feel now?

_____
_____
_____

Repeat this visualization daily for at least a week until you start to notice a shift in the intensity of the stories. You can draw on the same core stories or, if those start to feel softer, work with new ones. Remember that some stories will take longer to shift than others. Be patient. Also remember that we're not going for 100 percent resolution; that's the perfectionist's expectation, but it's not how healing works. We're looking for subtle shifts that, over time, lead to a more expanded sense internally.

If you have a tree nearby, I encourage you to write a copy of this core stories map and leave it at the base of the tree for a while—a few hours or more if you feel comfortable. If you have a photograph of the ancestor or a drawing of the imaginal ally, bring that along as well. The more you can visualize and embody laying down the stories, the more this practice will facilitate the process of interrupting patterns and laying down outdated stories.

Laying down stories can feel like laying down anxiety, as the two are directly correlated. What do you notice when you lay the stories down?

engage your mind

Boredom is one root cause of anxiety; if you don't engage your mind, it's more likely to default to anxiety. Many deeply curious people need their minds to be engaged as much as their hearts need to be nurtured. An engaged mind is a connected mind. Sphere by sphere, we root and connect and edge out anxiety.

Here are some signs of a bored/default mind and ways a mind could be engaged:

Default Mind	Engaged Mind
Worry	Study a language
Ruminations	Plant a garden
Scrolling	Create a recipe
Click and bait	Research an idea
Seeking reassurance	Read a book
Obsessions	Have interesting discussions
Intrusive thoughts	Listen to a podcast

Our minds can be used as a defense when we learn in younger years that it's safer to travel into the realm of thoughts and "lean to the left," as Daniel Siegel teaches, than it is to feel the enormity of emotions. This tendency to overthink as a way to avoid difficult feelings can serve us well in younger years, but eventually it stops serving us, and that's when we fall into a spiral of worry and intrusive thoughts.

But thinking isn't only a defense; our minds need to be stimulated in healthy ways. They need to sink into ideas that light them up. We talk a lot about "quieting the mind," which is essential, but our minds are also extraordinary tools for creativity, learning, and innovation when they're given the right attention.

When and how does your mind feel engaged? What do you watch, read, create, or listen to that is nourishing and life-enhancing? Feel free to look back on the questionnaire in the introduction for inspiration.

When do you find yourself in default mode—when your mind isn't engaged and anxiety takes hold? You might be able to identify this as times when you often turn to your phone to fill the emptiness. While scrolling can provide a temporary distraction, it doesn't usually address the anxiety at the root.

How might you engage your mind during these times? Sometimes when the type of anxiety that arises from emptiness takes hold, it's easy to forget about the things that fill it, so having it written down here can serve as your "cheat sheet." Then it's time to take action.

take a class or workshop

My grandparents were active learners until the ends of their lives. They were always enrolled in a class or two at their local community college, which not only provided an anchor for their week but kept their minds active. I lived in the apartment below their house for a year after I graduated from college, and I have vivid memories of watching them gather their school supplies every Tuesday morning. They returned invigorated and ready to discuss the subject of the class. There's so much to learn in this world, and our brains are designed to keep learning!

When is the last time you took a class or workshop just for fun (not for school or work)? If you've recently been in school, that might not sound appealing to you, but if it's been a while since you've been in a structured educational environment, consider taking a class or workshop on a subject that interests you.

Check any topics that ignite your mind. (You can explore a community college catalog or community events list to notice what lights you up and add your own.)

- Languages
- History
- Political science
- Current events
- Creative writing
- Literature
- Science
- Astronomy
- Economics
- Film and media studies
- Religious studies
- Art
- Physical practice or a sport
- _____
- _____

If possible, I encourage you to get into your community and try a class in person so you can both stimulate your mind and build connections with others, but of course online learning is also an option.

The more you ignite your mind and connect to others, the less anxious you feel.

How does the idea of taking a class or workshop make you feel?

What local class or workshop most excites you, and when might you take it?

stop ruminating by reading a poem

When we're stuck in anxiety, rumination, worry, and intrusive thoughts, we're trapped on the hamster wheel of the mind. The mind latches on to a self-critical thought or rumination and we gnaw on it until we chew the marrow out of our well-being. Nothing good comes from rumination, yet to simply "Stop ruminating" is easier said than done.

Instead, we can name it with kindness—*Oh, I just noticed that I'm ruminating*—then gently set aside the knotted topic and redirect your mind to something more life-affirming. One of my favorite ways to do this is to memorize a poem or prayer, then turn to it when I need to give my mind something nourishing to engage with.

→ **Use the following space to copy by hand or print out, then tape a favorite poem or prayer.*

Oftentimes when we're stuck on the hamster wheel, we forget how to get off of it. Having your poem here at the ready will help you replace the disconnect of rumination with the connection of poetry or prayer. Visually seeing your poem/prayer will also help you integrate it.

*If you don't have a favorite poem, I recommend anything from Mary Oliver, Ada Limón, Maya Angelou, David Whyte, or Pablo Neruda. And if you're open to poems that have a more religious or spiritual quality to them, I recommend the book *Love Poems from God* by Daniel Ladinsky.

one small text

Many of us fall into the habit of reaching for our phones when we have a spare moment. From the bathroom to the dining table, the phone has entered what was formally deemed sacred space. What are we searching for when we reach for the phone? A filler for boredom. A reprieve from loneliness. A dopamine hit. Again, I'm not anti-phone; it has its place and purpose, and I love my phone just as much as the next person. But quite often the impulse to reach and scroll comes from the desire to connect, yet it only leads to more disconnection. A thud of emptiness. And the more connected and nourished you are, the less anxious you'll be.

One simple way to replace the phone habit with a habit that is more connecting is to strategically place nourishing books in the places where you might normally reach for your phone: next to the toilet (yes!), where you normally eat (especially if you're eating alone), in your car or bag in case you find yourself waiting someplace unexpectedly, next to your bed, at your desk. Instead of texting, we can practice reaching for one small *actual* text.

One thoughtful text can ignite your mind, setting you on a course of reflection.

One small poem can fill your soul with nourishment and remind you of who you really are.

One short passage can anchor and connect you, reminding you of your place among things.

What is one place you could add a book or magazine?

_____

_____

_____

What books or magazines would you enjoy reading? (See the note on the next page if you'd like inspiration; a librarian could also offer suggestions.)

_____

_____

_____

Try using this strategy today, even just one time. How does it feel to reach for a book instead of the phone?

_____

_____

_____

Did you encounter any lines that lit you up? If so, record them here to refer to when anxiety threatens to take over.

_____

_____

_____

_____

_____

_____

*Here are some books I recommend. Many of them contain shorter passages or poems that are easy to read in a shorter amount of time. Please add your own to the list:

- *The Book of Awakening* by Mark Nepo
- *Simple Abundance* by Sarah Ban Breathnach
- *The Gift* by Hafiz
- Any books of poetry by Mary Oliver
- *The Book of Joy* by the Dalai Lama, Desmond Tutu, and Douglas Abrams
- *Love Poems from God* by Daniel Ladinsky

connecting to soul

One of the greatest disconnects of modern culture is our disproportionate emphasis on the realms of thinking, doing, deciphering, and understanding. We live in a neck-up culture, which means we give little time or credence to the underworld of being. We devalue the arts. We shove away feelings. We minimize the importance of slow time and doing nothing. These are all ways we deny the presence of soul. Yet when we deny the soul, it withers. We feel a great emptiness and dryness in our daily and nightly lives, and we seed the soil for anxiety to take root. Connection to soul is what makes us feel alive. It gives us energy, juice, and vitality. In a culture that devalues and denies the presence of soul and fails to honor soul-making activities, many people have forgotten how to connect to this place of vitality and meaning. This section will help you relearn how to water your soul.

connection and disconnection from our phones

One of our greatest modern culprits for disconnection is our phones.

Phones can be an assault to soul, especially during our more liminal—or in-between—times of day: morning when we first wake up, while eating, or just before bed. This is when the soul is more open and, thus, more vulnerable. We reach for the phone to assuage anxiety, but this temporary fix only amplifies anxiety in the long run. When we're more intentional about our phone use, anxiety abates.

We don't need to be perfectionists or purists in our phone use. Rather, I encourage you to gently notice how you feel about your phone, then take action on your own behalf to protect and preserve your soul when and how it makes sense for you.

Let's start by noticing how you feel when you reach for your phone at various times throughout the day versus reaching for something else.

How do you feel when you reach for your phone first thing in the morning?

I encourage you to leave your phone outside your bedroom at night so it's not the first thing you grab in the morning. For some people, this might sound impossible! Try to do it for just one night and morning and notice any differences in your nervous system and soul.

But . . . here's the important part: make a plan about what you will reach for instead of your phone.

Here are some ideas for alternatives to reaching for your phone:

- Say a short prayer or a few words of gratitude when you first wake up.

- Spend quality time with your pet or child without the phone in sight.

- Keep a journal beside your bed to write down a dream (more on dreams in part 3).

- Keep a book of poetry or prayer next to your bed and read a short entry.

- Keep a drawing pad and some pencils nearby so you can draw the tree outside your window or an image from a dream.

Let your soul guide you. One soulful act leads to the next. It's like placing nourishing layers of good food into the vessel of your soul.

Make your morning action plan here: what's the first thing you'll do when you wake up? And next?

1. _____

2. _____

3. _____

4. _____

5. _____

What do you notice when you're on your phone during meals?

What do you notice when you leave your phone in another space while you're eating and instead sit quietly, talk to a companion, or read a book?

What do you notice when you're on your phone at bedtime?

What do you notice when you put all screens away an hour before bed?

screen sabbath

I encourage you to try this challenging Gold Star Practice that connects to mind, heart, and soul and encourages you to connect to others in real time and real life: a twenty-four-hour screen sabbath. In many traditions, a sabbath is a sacred day of rest. In a screen sabbath, all screens are shut down for a full day and night, which includes phones, computers, tablets, and TVs. This may not sound like a soul-centered practice, but you might be amazed at what you experience when you consciously spend time away from these devices. I recommend trying this one time and noticing how you feel, then consider implementing it once a week or once a month.

Before your screen sabbath, consider your intentions for the day.

What are your hopes?

What are your fears or concerns?

Are there any people you'll need to inform about your sabbath and how they can reach you?

How will you spend your moments of downtime throughout the day and evening without your phone?

After your screen sabbath, I encourage you to reflect.
Was it challenging to shut down your phone?

How did it feel to have it off?

If you feel like this practice isn't for you, that can also be a valuable point of reflection. Also, you don't need to follow the practice exactly as I've described; you're free to experiment.
If a screen sabbath feels impossible, why?

Might you be able to adapt this practice to fit your life and needs?

the pause in your day

The soul lives on organic time or natural time. The pace of the natural world, the length of the seasons, the span of a single day and night have been the same since the beginning of time. There is a part of us, which we can call "soul," that still moves at this slower pace.

Our modern lives run on technological time, the pace of which is rapidly increasing. While it used to take months to deliver a letter, now we can send and receive communication in microseconds. Where we used to grow, harvest, and grind our own wheat and knead and bake it into bread, now we can order food or microwave a meal in minutes. Even books, a remnant of soulful living, can now be delivered to our devices in moments.

Technological time is helpful in many ways, but when we live *only* at the rapid pace of our modern lives, the soul is left behind. One way to recalibrate to organic time and, thus, connect to soul and reduce anxiety, is to take mindful pauses throughout a day. The pause is not a full-stop period, but a comma in our otherwise run-on sentence. As my *Gathering Gold* podcast cohost and niece, Victoria, once wrote: the pause is "a semicolon wink of awareness." When we remember to pause, we connect to soul, anchoring into one of our most accessible avenues for reconnection.

Here are some suggestions on **w**hen and h**ow** to pause. **N**otice **w**hich ones you're already doing and **w**hich ones you can imagine incorporating into your life.

Please add your own moments when you naturally pause or when you hope to add in a pause:

- Do one thing at a time. If you're cooking, just cook. If you're walking, just walk. And by all means if you're driving, just drive.

- Stop in the middle of a walk and notice where you are. If you're near a tree, notice the tree. We can become so hyper-focused on moving from point A to point B that we often forget to notice the scenery.

- Pause in the middle of a busy sidewalk! It's a very small act, but it's countercultural. It's subversive in the best possible way because it goes against our conditioning, and it's not something you normally see people do.

- Lie down on grass.

- Pause before leaving your place of employment, whether that's a home office or out in the world. Stand for thirty seconds in silence, and imagine releasing any parts of the day that you would like to leave behind.

- Notice the urge to fill in the natural pauses by reaching for your phone. Be curious about what lives in the empty spaces.

- Pause before getting into bed. Set aside time at night to look up at the sky and connect with the stars and moon in some way.

When will you pause today? What will be your cue to do so?

practice the pause with me

Now, let's take the pause out of theory and into action right now, with me, in this moment.

It takes courage to pause because we never know what we're going to meet. Might we find grief? A painful memory? Last night's dream? Even joy, which many people struggle to let in? It's a lot easier and safer to keep going.

But, again, the pause feeds the soul. We need it like we need food and water. Once we shift our habitual resistance to pausing, it becomes a lot less scary. And one way to shift is to hold hands and pause together. As Piglet says (the quintessential character of the anxious mind), "It's so much more friendly with two."

> **Take a one-minute pause with me right now. Set your timer for sixty seconds and just sit, just be, wherever you are.**

Now that you've paused, notice what came up for you.

_____
_____
_____
_____

Did the pause feel nourishing? Annoying? Easy? Difficult? There are no right or wrong answers.

_____
_____
_____

Write or draw anything that emerged from your soul below.

For more on the pause, I encourage you to check out the *Gathering Gold* podcast episode called "The Power of the Pause," particularly the moment (at minute twenty-three) where Victoria and I take a pause together and share what we notice.

pause and poetry

When we pause, we open to the possibility of inviting in ordinary magic: noticing bright stars against a black sky, noticing the sound of crunchy snow or leaves beneath our feet. It's what poets and artists know, for there is no poetry without noticing, and there is no noticing without a pause. Art is one of the soul's most nourishing foods.

> **As you pause, open to a poem, an image, a few words, colors, or any other form of creativity. Record it here as a reminder of the power of the pause to connect you to your soul.**

If nothing creative arrives, that's okay. Emptiness is the necessary precursor to creativity, and sometimes our souls need to rest in the fallow place of nothingness before the new birth arrives. Make room for that as well without judgment, and trust that a moment of "nothing" is also deeply nourishing for the soul.

visualization to cleanse and release

Just as the mind needs to be engaged, so the soul longs for connection. One way we can meet this need is to enter imaginal space where we're guided in a gentle and poetic way. When we're guided by someone we trust, the soul feels held and anxiety often recedes.

In this visualization, I'm going to guide you into an imaginal ritual where you can purify and cleanse in living waters, waters that are infused with life energy that will help you let go of what is no longer needed in all four realms of self: body, heart, mind, and spirit. Ideally, we would walk to an actual lake or creek, but since many of us don't have access to those places, we will travel to the bodies of water in our minds.

I recommend doing this visualization when you have time and space to drop in and down to your heart and body. If it helps you to drop in, I suggest lighting a candle.

An audio recording of this visualization is available at:

soundstrue.com/the-healing-anxiety-workbook-bonus

How did you feel during the visualization?

_____
_____
_____
_____
_____

How do you feel now?

_____
_____
_____
_____
_____

dreamwork

One powerful and nourishing way to connect with our souls is to work with our dreams. Everyone dreams, which means everyone has access to this often untapped treasure trove of wisdom, guidance, nourishment, and creativity. If you have a hard time remembering your dreams, I recommend you keep a journal next to your bed, avoid opening your eyes right away when you wake up, and actively search for the tail end of your dream. With enough intention, you will likely start to follow the breadcrumbs of a dream, but even a dream snippet can contain worlds of food for the soul.

    Most people rush through their mornings so quickly that they ignore their dreams, which, as the Talmud says, is like leaving a letter from soul unopened. As many of us don't grow up valuing the potency of dreams, we tend to invalidate their power. But the soul knows. And when we take just a few minutes in the mornings to be with our dreams in some way, the soul's hunger starts to be satiated and anxiety is edged out. As Jill Mellick writes in *The Art of Dreaming*: "The food of and for the soul is our imagination. When we do not feed the soul, we die a little."

The most powerful—and fun!—way I know to work with dreams is to approach them creatively. There is no single meaning of dream imagery, and Googling our dreams doesn't feed the soul, which asks to be seen and related to.

Instead of trying to interpret a dream, I invite you to play with a few ways of working with them.

First, recall a recent dream or a dream snippet and write it down in as much detail as you can.

Now, draw one image from the dream:

Next, play with recording the dream as a poem. This isn't about writing a "beautiful" poem; it's simply a way to relate to the dream from a different, more flexible part of your brain:

Finally, meditate on the strongest image from the dream and embody it as a gesture, then draw the gesture here. By "gesture," I mean a physical movement that expresses some aspect of the image. For example, if you dreamed of the moon, you might make the gesture of a circle with your arms.

dream mandala

Mandalas are one of my favorite ways of working not only with dreams, but with accessing and communicating with the unconscious in all realms of life. *Mandala* is Sanskrit for "circle," and mandalas have been used for centuries in cultures around the world as a way to connect to our root and center. A mandala invites us to concretize and contain our inner world through artistic expression. Because it's a circular form, it naturally invites us to step into the right hemisphere of the brain, which is our more creative, nonlinear side. Many of us live in a left-hemisphere-dominant culture that values linear thinking, problem-solving, facts, and definite answers over imagination, creativity, possibility, and mystery. Every time we access the right hemisphere, we connect with the soul sphere on the Tree of Life. The soul is starving for imagination and possibility, and working with dreams feeds this hunger. When this hunger is satiated, anxiety quiets down.

> Creating a mandala is **q**uite straightforward. Thin**k** of a dream or a snippet of a dream. **U**sing the template, **fi**ll in the four sections **w**ith images, colors, and/or **w**ords from your dream.

Don't overthink it; kindly walk your perfectionist to the door! The goal here is not to create "great art"; we're simply drawing on an ancient form to give containment and expression to the images of a dream. You don't even need to think directly about the dream as you're allowing the images to flow out of you onto the page. In fact, the less you think (left brain), the more readily you'll access your right brain. Come back to this page whenever you need an infusion of soul food. Just looking at what you created will fill your soul.

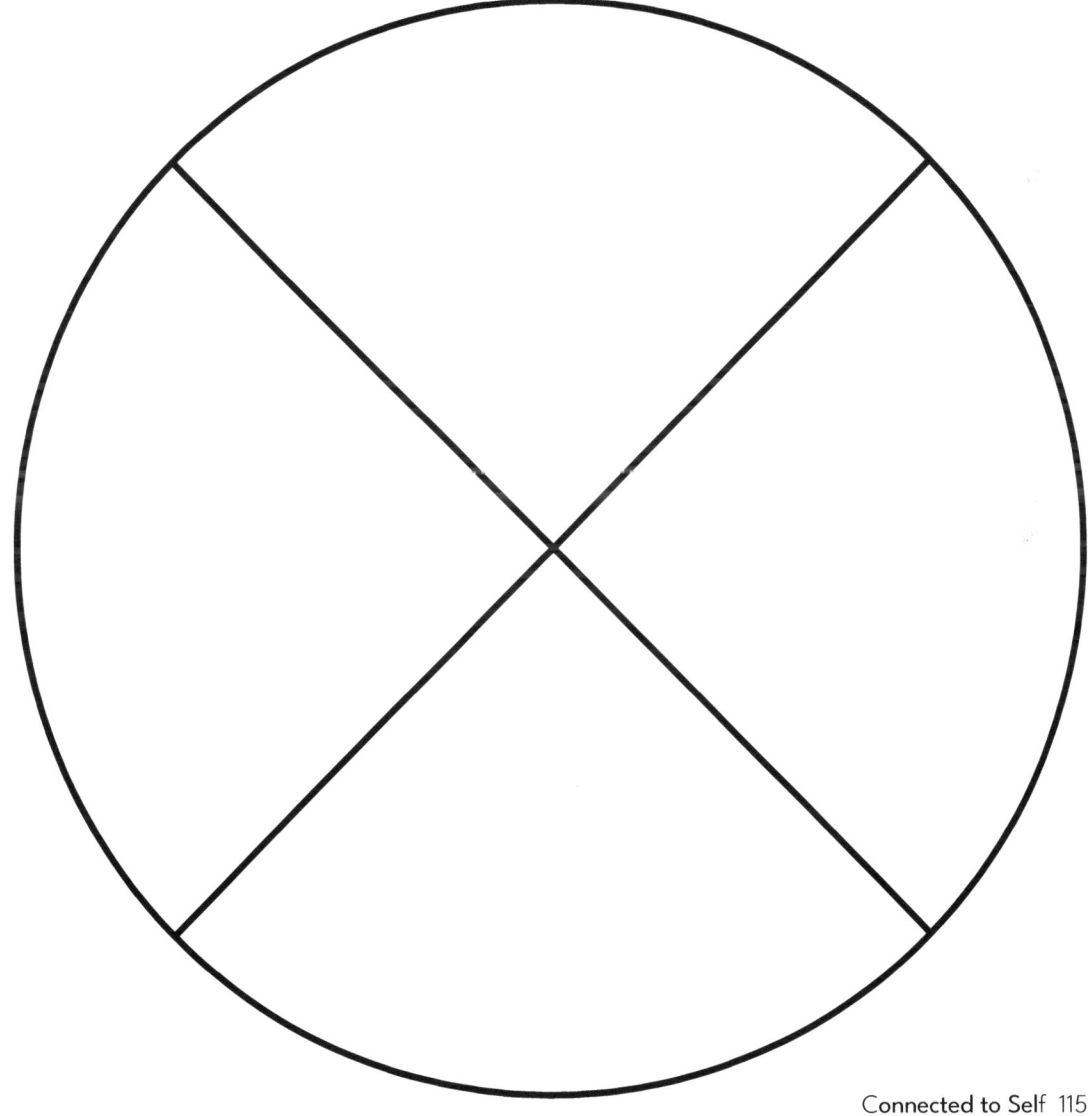

We need each other. It's not enough to have a deep connection to ourselves. We are social animals, and we need to be connected to others in order to feel safe in this world. Everyone has different social needs. Some people need a big group of friends, while others feel content with just a few good friends. As we enter this section, we want to be mindful of societal expectations around partnership, family, and friendship so we can watch for the shame-based voice of comparison that might arise. I will be naming these in each section.

part two

connected to others

connecting to friends, family, partner, animals

The first sphere of the right side of the Tree of Life contains our connections with others who are closest to us: people and animals we see daily or regularly. These are the connections that infuse us with a deep sense of belonging. While some people are more solitary, most of us are biologically wired to be in close connection to others. Like wolves, we are pack animals. That doesn't mean you don't need time alone, especially if you're an introvert. But it means that you recognize that part of your well-being and safety comes from being in your "pack" or your "puppy pile."

That said, a pack or puppy pile can also be fraught with pain, and you might struggle with societal expectations about how friendship or family is "supposed" to look. Let me remind you: there are no "shoulds." Many cultural messages assert that everyone needs a big group of friends or a "best friend," and that social connection is contingent upon going to parties or big social gatherings. This might serve some people's extroverted needs, but it's certainly not for everyone. Similarly, you might not have a close connection with your biological family or you might not be in a romantic relationship, and this can bring grief or longing. We want to make room for the pain—trying the exercises in the Heart section can help—while also moving toward our personal template for social connections.

There is no right way to be connected to others. If this is a sphere of more disconnect for you, meet that disconnect with compassion, know that you're far from alone with your longing, and harness your Wise Self/Inner Parent to consider ways to grow your circle of connection to others.

non-human friends

If you're blessed enough to live with non-human animals, you know very well how quickly they can connect you to your heart, your joy, and to an overall sense of well-being. Animal friends are divine gifts in this world, and sometimes it only takes a few minutes of connecting with your furry, feathery, or scaly friend to shift from a closed heart to an open heart. They return us to a state of *being* instead of staying on the constant treadmill of *doing* that our culture encourages. Anxiety is a ruminative headspace, so when we drop out of our heads and into our bodies, anxiety often abates.

As Eckhart Tolle so beautifully writes in *Guardians of Being: Spiritual Teachings from Our Dogs and Cats*, "Just watching an animal closely can take you out of your mind and bring you into the present moment, which is where the animal lives all the time—surrendered to life . . . When you pet a dog or listen to a cat purring, thinking may subside for a moment and a space of stillness arises within you, a doorway to Being."

Let's recognize the role that pets have played in your life by creating a two-dimensional altar where you can offer gratitude for your animal friends.

As I write these words, our cat, Tashi, is sitting next to me on the top of the couch, bathed in shimmery sunlight and interrupting my writing with her requests for attention, which I'm happy to oblige. Not a day passes when I don't worship at the altar of her paws and thank the great gods of nature for the existence of cats. Likewise, my first dog, Duchess, a German shepherd, guarded me as a baby and was my best friend as a toddler. In fact, my very first word was "utch," an indicator of how deeply embedded into my heart she was.

Who are your animal friends? These might be animals that have lived in your home or other animals you've connected with. Even if you haven't had pets, most of us have had a special connection with an animal at some point in our lives.

Use the space below to tape or glue a photo of each animal who has made a difference in your life, then write a bit about them.

If you don't have a photo, do your best to draw the animal.

a friendship tree

Our culture elevates romantic love as the pinnacle of relationships. While many people are drawn to committed intimate relationships, it's equally important to remember the immeasurable value of friendship. Nurturing our friendships is part of what makes us feel whole, alive, and connected. Friendship is an act of belonging, and belonging is one of the elements that makes us feel attached, safe, and rooted in this life.

When we feel the safety that arises from belonging, anxiety abates.

Honor your friends throughout your life in the form of a friendship tree. Sometimes a friend enters your life for a season, and it can be painful when the friendship ends, but it's important to honor this friend as contributing to the fullness of this particular sphere on the Tree of Life. This exercise is especially important if you carry a story that says, *I don't have enough friends.* When you spend time reflecting on friendship over your lifespan, you will likely see a longer story that can help you reshape how friendship lives inside of you. However, if pain or longing arises, please make space for that as well.

Find a comfortable place and close your eyes if that helps you to turn inward. Gently, without strain or effort, begin to fly back through the years to your earliest memory of friendship. Perhaps it was a friend in your neighborhood, at preschool, or in kindergarten (0–5 years old). Continue your time travel as you traverse through elementary school (5–11 years), middle school (11–14 years), and high school (14–18 years). Follow memory to places other than school where you found friendship: summer camp, afterschool classes, sports, religious centers, and later, work, classes, or through other friends. Then, travel into your twenties and continue through the decades until you arrive at present day.

→ For each stage of life, **write down who you remember and a few words**, phrases, or images that come to mind a**b**out each person. This is your friendship tree.

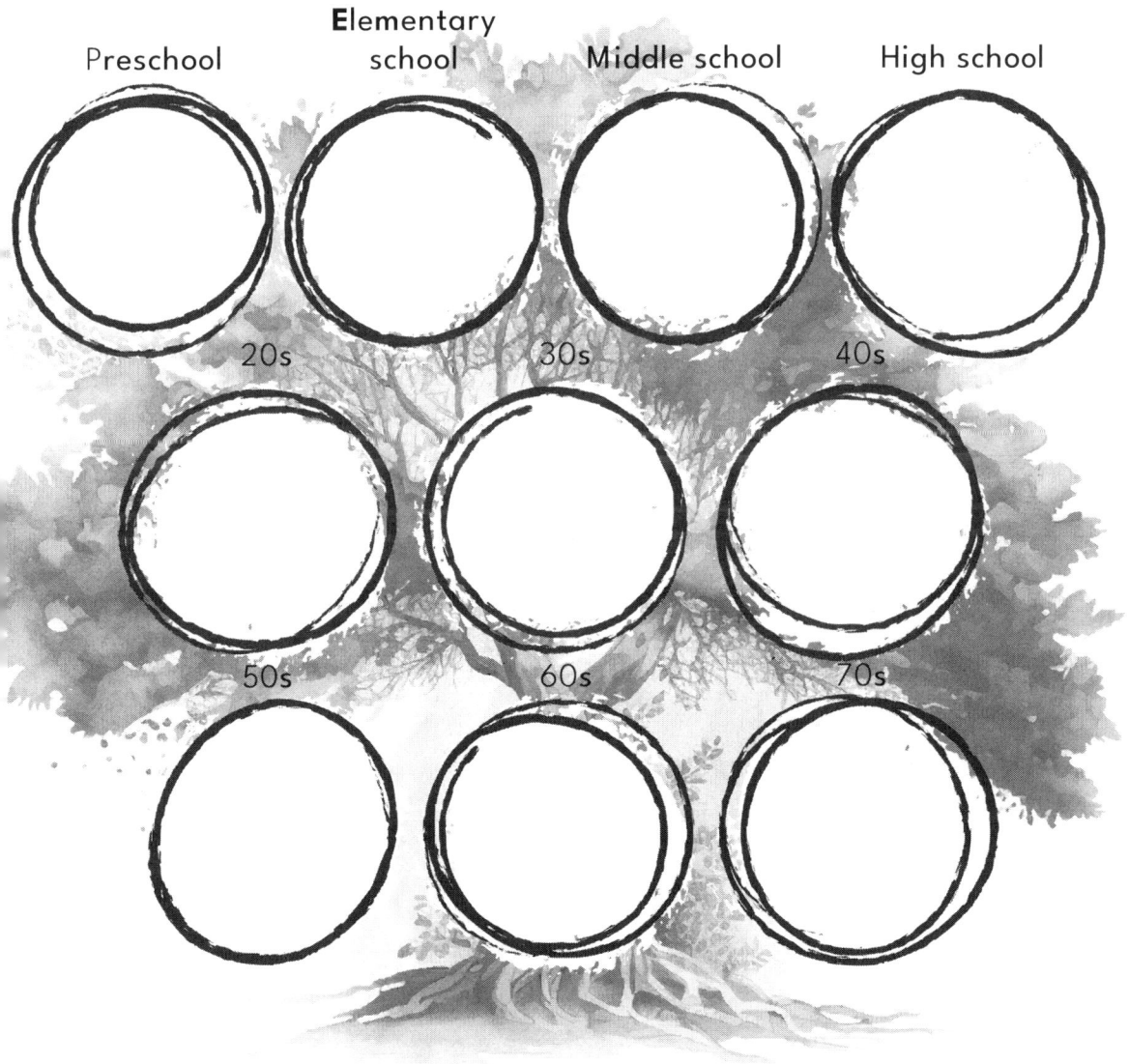

Preschool | Elementary school | Middle school | High school

20s | 30s | 40s

50s | 60s | 70s

partner gratitude

Note: If you are not currently in a committed partnership, please skip this exercise. Notice feelings that may arise if you're single and hoping to be in a relationship. Return to the Heart section to attend to any grief, longing, or loneliness that may be present.

Many people today expect their committed relationship to fulfill the needs that an entire community used to meet. The expectation is too high, for the truth is we all need multiple sources of human connection: family, friends, neighbors, colleagues. Nevertheless, since partnership carries so much weight, let's take some time to honor it here.

The most effective way I know to honor our partners is through daily gratitude lists. We will revisit gratitude again in the section on spiritual connection, but since gratitude is one of our most effective elixirs against anxiety, you can never have too much of it.

Bring your partner to your mind's eye and think about all of the ways you appreciate them. Be both general and specific. For example, a specific appreciation is: *I'm so grateful that my partner shoveled the driveway this morning in subfreezing temperatures.*

A general gratitude might sound like: *I'm grateful that my partner doesn't complain when we visit my family.*

Use the following lines to make a gratitude list that can serve as a template for a regular habit that can hopefully find its way into a regular practice.

This practice is best done daily or weekly.

1.
2.
3.
4.
5.
6.
7.
8.
9.
10.

family stories

The family we're raised in forms our first points of connection. For some, these points of connection are sources of safety, love, and belonging. For others, they're a source of pain. And for most, they include both love and pain, for, when it comes to human relationships, these two elements often intersect in the rooms of the heart. If your original family unit was toxic, you may have chosen to create distance and direct your need for family toward a "heart family" or chosen family.

Reflecting on family members who were or are sources of safety strengthens your sense of belonging and reminds you that you're not alone.

Belonging = Attachment
Attachment = Safety
Safety reduces anxiety.

One of the most effective ways to reflect is to tell stories.

I invite you to tell a story about someone from your family who made you feel safe in your early years and a family member in your current stage of life who brings a sense of warmth when you think about them.

This might sound like, *I remember playing imaginary games in the backyard with my sister,* or *I feel so happy to be reconnecting with my cousin in Chicago.*

Tell a heartwarming story about a family member in your growing-up years:

Tell a heartwarming story about a family member in your current life:

connecting to local community

There's a particular safety that happens when we're connected to neighbors and our local community. Knowing and trusting that our neighbors are there for us and we're there for them, even if they're not our closest friends, taps us into our most primal need to live in community. In an ideal world, a neighborhood is a built-in network of connections; when we connect with the people living within eye- and earshot, we feel held and safe in a special way. Sadly, these days we don't always make time to connect with our local community. But what we can name, we can change, and when we recognize the importance of these connections, we can prioritize them with time and attention.

the connectivity of neighbors

Studies show that altruism rose dramatically in 2020 during the first peak of the COVID crisis, especially in neighborhoods: neighbors helping people with mobility or health challenges by offering to bring groceries and pick up medication; neighbors expressing gratitude to city workers, like sanitation workers; people who had never spoken to each other having time to sit on the balcony and talk about the day.

I'll never forget when, in the first days of lockdown, I called my neighbor in a slight panic after returning from the grocery store where I had seen rows of empty shelves. Would there be enough food? She assured me there would and then said, with her Southern warmth and grit, "If we have to catch crawdads from the creek, we will. We're not going to let anyone starve around here." I burst into tears of relief and solidarity. Whatever was going to happen, we would endure it together. My anxiety calmed down instantly.

People tend to band together during hardship, but we don't have to wait for disaster to strike to make neighborly connections. If you're an introvert, it might be more difficult to find the courage to make these connections, but the effort is well worth it.

What stands out for you as you read about neighborly connections?

_____
_____
_____
_____
_____

On a scale of 1–5, how satisfied do you feel with your connections to neighbors?

          1   2   3   4   5

If you notice some pangs of longing for deeper connections, explore your feelings here.

_____
_____
_____
_____
_____

Which neighbors do you currently feel connected to?

_____
_____
_____

Which neighbors do you wish for more connection with? Or a different type of connection?

_____

_____

_____

Ideas for ways to initially connect with neighbors:

- Say hello when you're out on a walk. If a neighbor is walking with a dog, ask if you can pet the dog.
- Wave when you're driving by.
- Make connections through your local Nextdoor group.
- If you have an elderly neighbor, offer to help bring in their groceries.

Ideas for ways to deepen connections with neighbors:

- Suggest a book club with a few people with whom you've made a connection.
- Ask a neighbor to take a walk.
- Start a monthly game night.
- Ask a couple of neighbors if they would like to host a block party with you.

community connections

The gym, the coffee shop, the grocery store, the library . . . these are some of the locations in our communities where we can make small yet meaningful points of connection.

There's a reason why many people, myself included, prefer to work out at a gym rather than at home. Why? Because when we can tap into the community energy of many people running or lifting, we feel connected and inspired. There's a connectivity that happens when we work out together that encourages all of us to keep going. I'm an introvert, but I'm also a people person and I love people-watching. I love seeing the older couple on the stationary bikes with their flash cards (I've been wanting to ask them for weeks what they're studying). I love seeing the women in my age range making the commitment to take care of their bodies. I love seeing the kids working out with their parents. It's life-affirming. And it's community.

I've also enjoyed the more personal connections I make. When the faces I see every week are matched to names, I feel joy. Connection. And there's a particular tenor to the joy when they greet me by name. Recognition. A small but important moment of belonging. These smaller moments of connection add up to widen the pool of safety that absorbs anxiety.

Held in the larger web, we feel safer and anxiety calms.

Sometimes we overlook community connections, but it's important to notice and name them so we can underscore the ways we're linked.

 Check which points of connection apply, then use the space to expand on these ways you feel connected to your local community.

I have connections:

- ○ At the coffee shop
- ○ At a restaurant
- ○ At my kid's school
- ○ On the bus (subway, train, etc.)
- ○ At the bus stop
- ○ At the gym
- ○ At the grocery store
- ○ At the post office
- ○ At the library

Do you long for more local connection? What might that look like, and what does it feel like?

widening the circle

When our older son was two years old, we moved from Los Angeles to Colorado, leaving behind a strong group of friends. As an introvert, I knew it would take me time to make new friends, but I had no idea it would take as long as it took. I felt like an outsider in our neighborhood for many years, and I had a hard time finding my place in a spiritual community. In our younger years, we often meet people in school and work environments, but when we move through our twenties and enter our thirties, the circles often become smaller.

Ten years after we moved, I had a dream that I was in a circle of women led by my rabbi. Gathering my courage, I asked her if she would be willing to lead a monthly spiritual circle, and to my great joy, she said yes. For years, that group was an anchor and strong point of connection. Eventually, our rabbi needed to move on to other projects, but a few of us have kept the group going on our own, and it continues to be one of the most nourishing parts of our month.

Friendship can come in many forms.

→ **We need to connect with people who have shared values and interests, and there are many ways to do that.**

Making new connections requires taking the risk to be vulnerable and confront any social anxiety that arises. If social anxiety is something you struggle with on a regular basis, please consider seeking support. (I also have blog posts and a podcast episode on this topic.) Good friends aren't likely to come knocking on your door; you have to seek them!

How do you feel about your current circle of connections?

___

___

Are you open to widening it? If so, how might you do so?

___

___

Here are some ideas for how to widen your circle:

- Join a Meetup group that orients around a common interest (hiking, skiing, writing dreamwork, dancing).

- Join or start a book club.

- Join an online app, specifically for making friends, like Bumble For Friends.

- Search for local New Moon or Full Moon groups. You can find local moon circles here: meetup.com/topics/moon-circles/.

- If you are a male, you can find both online and local men's groups here: https://mkpusa.org/mens-group.

"Rather than a heroic journey undertaken by a select few, the genius myth imagines that everyone, by virtue of bearing some genius qualities, is subject to a genuine calling in life. The question becomes not whether or not you are a genius, but in what way does genius appear in you and how might it contribute to both your own well-being and that of the world around you . . . In the same way that each infant arrives with a unique set of fingerprints as well as precise brain printing, each soul bears an inner imprint and unique psychic pattern."

—**Michael Meade,** ***The Genius Myth***

connecting to purpose

Purpose is connection to the greater fabric of humanity. It gives life meaning, and meaning is an integral part of the connective tissue that makes us feel alive. The more alive we feel, the less room there is for anxiety to take root.

Purpose is more powerful than anxiety.

For some people, purpose might be a more solitary endeavor, like living in nature far from others and being called to tend to the land. But, for many of us, purpose is interwoven into our connection to other humans, which is why it lives on the right side of the Tree of Life: Others. We create art, and we long for the art to be seen. We make food, and we need the food to be appreciated and eaten by others. We are teachers, baristas, therapists, lawyers, podcasters, writers, grocery store clerks, thinkers, parents, office workers. We offer our gifts, and the gifts are received. This process of giving and receiving is part of the infinity loop that connects us to the whole.

what's your soulprint?

Most of us yearn to contribute to the fabric of society in a meaningful way. When we don't feel purposeful, anxiety finds a way to seep into that crack.

We tend to think of purpose and contribution as only being connected to our employment. Often this is the case, but it's not the only way we feel purposeful. How about the parent who devotes their life to raising their children but never receives a paycheck? Or the adult-child in midlife who chooses to take care of their elderly parent? Or the devoted volunteer? There are many ways to bring our full selves, the heart of who we are, into this world.

One way to consider how we contribute is by identifying the unique qualities of our soulprint. Just like we all have a fingerprint and a brainprint, we also have a soulprint. Let's pause here to take that in: *every person on this planet has their own unique prints that define their physical, mental, and spiritual personhood.* Of course, we can't see a soulprint under a microscope, but when we look closely enough, we know it's there.

What, exactly, is a soulprint? Riffing on Michael Meade's quote in the introduction to this section, I'm going to define it as: the unique pattern that contains the essence of who you are and longs to be shared with others. Let's get curious about the underlying threads that comprise the soul-tapestry of who we are.

When asked to list their intrinsic qualities, most people draw a blank. This incredible list, adapted from the book *All Children Flourishing* by Howard Glasser, can offer inspiration.

Read through and check any qualities that apply to you.

These may be basic qualities that you always possess or qualities that reveal themselves in a specific situation like, *Oh, I was very gracious today when my husband brought his colleague home from work unexpectedly. I love that I was so flexible.*

Glasser encourages you to, "Tell your child that he or she is . . ." But I'm changing it to:

"Tell yourself that you are . . ."

- ○ A joy
- ○ A good friend
- ○ A hard worker
- ○ A source of strength
- ○ A leader
- ○ A light
- ○ A helper
- ○ An advocate
- ○ Aware
- ○ Accomplishing a lot

- ○ Admirable
- ○ Appreciative
- ○ Attentive
- ○ Bringing out the best in others
- ○ Compassionate
- ○ Considerate
- ○ Cooperative
- ○ Creative
- ○ Courageous
- ○ Clear

- ○ Committed
- ○ Courteous
- ○ Diligent
- ○ Discerning
- ○ Direct
- ○ Dignified
- ○ Easy to like
- ○ Efficient
- ○ Empathetic
- ○ Flexible
- ○ Focused
- ○ Forgiving
- ○ Generous
- ○ Going above and beyond
- ○ Gracious
- ○ Good-hearted
- ○ Having an open mind
- ○ Honorable
- ○ Hopeful
- ○ Independent
- ○ Inspiring

- ○ Inquisitive
- ○ Intelligent
- ○ Just and fair
- ○ Kind
- ○ Loving
- ○ Looking out for others
- ○ Organized
- ○ Open-minded
- ○ Patient
- ○ Positive
- ○ Productive
- ○ Passionate
- ○ Reasonable
- ○ Respectful
- ○ Responsible
- ○ Seeing the big picture
- ○ Steadfast
- ○ Trustworthy
- ○ Thankful
- ○ Understanding
- ○ Vibrant
- ○ Visionary

↗ **A**dd your **ow**n inspired appreciations here:

_____
_____
_____
_____
_____

Once you have reviewed your wonderful qualities, take a moment to express appreciation to yourself now:

_____
_____
_____
_____
_____

Review this list and express appreciation to yourself as a regular practice.

the myth of a calling

One of the insidious pressures that causes people to shy away from living out their soulprint is the myth of a calling. Many of us hear cultural messages that say: "If you're not living out your dream career, you're settling. Follow your bliss! Live your dreams! The world is your oyster! Go make it happen!"

But it's not as black-and-white as that. There is a real issue of being able to support yourself financially, and the fact of the matter is many jobs offer stability, while "following your bliss" is often a riskier endeavor. There's immense pressure to "live up to your potential," which is a phrase that often causes unnecessary anxiety.

 **To calm this anxiety, let's reframe how we relate to work—whether it's paid or unpaid.**

Are you contributing to society in a positive way?

_____

_____

_____

What moments in your day can you exercise choice and autonomy—even if these moments are small?

Does your work or the way you spend your days bring you some satisfaction?

Do you spend your days with people with whom you feel connected? If so, reflect on how this feels and how it contributes to your sense of connection and belonging.

What benefits do you get from your work, be it paid or unpaid? What gratitude might you feel for these benefits?

the gifts that are longing to be seen

We all have latent gifts that we keep hidden because it feels too vulnerable to share them. This simple yet powerful exercise will help you name those gifts and begin to bring them into the open, if only on this page. There is unseen power in writing things down, and an even greater power when we surround the writing with images. This exercise will help you begin to claim your unseen gifts and amplify their goodness.

Remember: the gifts you refer to aren't necessarily about your job but about the gifts that you're hoping to bring more fully into the world in some way. These are your sparks.

**The more sparks you connect to,
the less room there is for anxiety.
Sparks are joy, and joy is stronger than fear.**

→ Think about the gifts you keep hidden but are longing to bring into the world. The following are the most common that I hear with my clients. Check all that apply:

Though it might not be evident from the outside, inside I am a . . .

- ○ Writer
- ○ Musician
- ○ Singer
- ○ Gardener
- ○ Chef
- ○ Poet
- ○ Podcaster
- ○ Blogger
- ○ Dancer
- ○ Artist
- ○ _____
- ○ _____

↗ **Now write the words that sparkle for you in the boxes below and on the next page.**

Get out your crayons or markers and make each box colorful. This isn't about great art. It's about honoring these latent gifts and making them feel alive. Spend time looking at the boxes every morning. Release any pressure to take action. This is just about gently bringing more of your soulprint into your awareness so you can feel more comfortable with the gifts of you.

we cannot save the whole world

When we talk about purpose, we can tip into an anxious trigger around the question of "enough": *Am I doing enough to save our planet? Am I doing enough to contribute to society? Am I doing enough to create more equality and justice?*

I, too, have struggled with these questions. But then I come back to this reminder:

We must only do what we are called to do, the things we do well, the origin of passion.

Our only task is to tend to these domains, not the whole world, not the places that arise from "should" and do not belong to us.

Water the garden of our gifts and bring these into our aching world.

That is all. And it is enough.

When we water the garden of our gifts, it is enough.

When we rest, it is enough.

I want to be very clear that identifying your purpose doesn't mean you are responsible for the entire world. It doesn't mean you have to work harder and submit to grind culture. In fact, I think it means the opposite. It means trusting in your rhythm, in your need for rest and nourishment, in the value of sitting and witnessing the world around you without needing to transpose that witnessing into any *thing*, even a thing as lovely as a poem or a song.

For some people, their gift may be more in the *being* than the *doing*, more in singing near a creek than writing a song for human ears.

Most of us, I believe, vacillate between rhythms of outward and inward, busy and calm, expressive and silent. And we may have seasons where we are allowing the inner landscapes to lie fallow and replenish without needing to generate and create.

Finding your genius or soulprint doesn't mean running out and changing your entire life. It doesn't mean getting busier and more frantic. It means looking for the through lines, the threads that have run through your life, and following them gently and slowly into the expression of who you really are. This is what the world needs: a quiet burgeoning of the essence of you.

Saying a mantra, phrase, or short poem that reminds you that you are enough and you are doing enough when the anxiety of "not enough" seeps in can help you realign and reconnect.

Check any of the following that resonate with you and commit one or two to memory so you can come back to it when you're feeling like you're not enough:

○ I am enough.

○ I am worthy.

○ I am plenty.

If you're connected to your lineage, I recommend finding out how to say "I am enough" in a language your family has spoken. There's a particular power in hearkening back to our ancestry when we're changing old patterns around scarcity and abundance.

- Dayenu (Hebrew for "It is enough")

- Ní beag dom féin mé ("I am enough for myself" in Gaelic)

- Yo soy suficiente ("I am enough" in Spanish)

There is a world both beyond this one and intricately interwoven into it. It's the world of the ancestors, of creativity and spirituality, of nature. We can't see the ancestors, but we know we're still connected to them, even though they departed from this plane long ago. We can't place the creative spirit under a microscope, but we know the feeling of inspiration when we're touched by it. And while we *can* see the natural world, we can't see the feelings we derive when we're connected to it.

Many of us are conditioned to be skeptical about these realms, and we're taught to value the intellect over the unseen worlds. We spend years and sometimes decades in school learning about math, literature, science, and history without taking a single class on the importance of connecting to our ancestors or the comfort and calm that arise through our connections to nature. This is a tragic deficit in our education system, and the result is an increasing disconnect from the realms that have soothed and guided humans for thousands of years. If we're going to calm anxiety at the root, we need to reconnect to these touchstones that attach us to some of our most powerful places of belonging.

part three

connected to the unseen

connecting to ancestors

One of the many deficits in the rationalist-materialist culture many of us live in is that we've lost touch with the ancestral realm. We may be open to connecting with our family stories or recipes—as we'll do in this section—but when it comes to speaking directly with a departed relative, doubt might set in. Yet, in many cultures around the world and throughout history, honoring and conversing with departed ones is a regular part of life. In these cultures, there's an implicit understanding that when we lose touch with the ancestral realm, we cut ourselves off from the connective tissues that run through our lives. Conversely, when we make contact with the dead, a broken link is restored. We feel this connection in our souls. We have a sense that we've returned to a birthright of belonging, and our breath deepens.

family stories and history

We all come from somewhere, and the stories of our history comprise the threads of one of our most ancient tapestries of connection. In other times, our family lore would have been passed down through the generations: stories told by the fire during winter or around the stove while cooking with female relatives or out in the field while planting the new crops. But, in our fast-paced and increasingly disconnected culture, there seems to be less time for storytelling. As such, many of us have lost the threads of where we come from, which leads to a feeling of disconnect and anxiety.

> One **way to repair is to b**egin to **fi**ll in the gaps through research. Start **b**y writing down as much of your family story as you **k**now.

If you don't know much, do some research. This can be your blood family or, if you're adopted, the family that raised you. Ask relatives. Be curious. If you know very little, sign up for a free trial with ancestry.com. Even if you're disconnected from your family, this can still be a connective exercise, as there are positive stories in every family, even amidst the pain or trauma.

If this task feels daunting, start with one relative and one story. Recently, I reached out to an older second cousin to ask about her mother, who was my grandfather's sister. It was a very simple request: "Please tell me about your mom!" Most relatives love to recount stories from their past, so the conversation itself is often a nourishing one.

What have you learned about the story of your family?

family recipes

Food is one of our most accessible sources of connection, belonging, and love. For many caregivers, food was a love language; your grandmother may not have told you very often that she loved you, but every time you visited, she filled you up with her delicious recipes. Or perhaps holidays were when time-honored family recipes would find their way to the table. Whenever I ask my husband what we should make for Christmas Eve dinner, he says, "Baked ziti!" And when we make it, his Italian roots and family memory find their way to our Coloradan table. Recipes from our families are often interwoven with our heritage, and it's these connections that link us back through the centuries and help us remember that we are part of something bigger than ourselves.

What are some of your favorite family recipes? List them here:

1. _____
2. _____
3. _____
4. _____
5. _____

Now take some time to write down, by hand, a favorite family recipe. If you have a recipe in a family's member handwriting, consider photocopying it and pasting it below. This small point of connection will likely fill you with joy, and joy is more powerful than anxiety.

ask an ancestor to take your worry

Can you imagine how much less lonely, disconnected, and anxious you would feel if you knew and trusted that there were beings all around you waiting to help you navigate your life, keep you and your loved ones safe, and guide you toward the fulfillment of your dreams? And all you had to do was ask for help and they would be there? As Perdita Finn writes in *Take Back the Magic: Conversations with the Unseen World*, "I call on the dead when I'm fretting in the middle of the night. I call on the dead when I'm worried, anxious, concerned, helpless, and overwhelmed. And they always answer. They always let me know they are there."

The way I conceptualize ancestral prayer work is that even if there are no ancestors in another realm, focusing on life-affirming conversations is much more calming than staying stuck in worry. It's simply a better place to put our energy. We can choose to stay stuck in worry, or we can choose to ask an ancestor to hold our worry for us, thereby helping us to get off the worry treadmill and get on with our day.

Let's imagine that ancestors with whom you feel some connection are standing by, waiting for you to ask them for specific help. This can be on a smaller scale, like *Please help my son find his clarity of mind and his confidence during his math test today.* Or it can be on a larger scale, like *Please be with my mother as she endures cancer treatment.* From what I understand about ancestral work, all of your ancestors are available to help you, even those whom you didn't know. This means you can extend as far back into your family history as you feel called as you develop connections with departed ones. You can also call upon departed loved ones you felt kinship with, even if you weren't blood related.

Every time you notice worry, transmute it into a request for help. Fill in the blanks below.

My worry is: _____

My request to my ancestor/loved one [fill in their name] is: _____

_____

My worry is: _____

My request to my ancestor/loved one [fill in their name] is: _____

_____

My worry is: _____

My request to my ancestor/loved one [fill in their name] is: _____

_____

offer gratitude to ancestors

Every Indigenous culture knows what many people today have forgotten: the ancestors need to be nourished. We can nourish them with food offerings (for example, leaving a small glass of milk or a small bowl of food out for them) and/or we can nourish them with gratitude.

One of my favorite ancestor practices is to sit in front of my altar of photos and thank each person for something specific that they gave me. For example:

> "Grandma Sarah: Thank you for crossing the Atlantic Ocean when you were twelve years old. Your courage and fortitude gave us the opportunity for a better life. Thank you for your strength."

> "Grandpa Izzy: Thank you for the Zapota malted you would make for me from the tree in your garden! Thank you for all of the fresh fruits and vegetables from your garden and for your love of gardening, which you passed on to me. Thank you for taking us camping every summer and keeping us safe. Thank you for your mischievous smile that would light up every time your grandkids walked in the door."

You get the picture!

Of course, this will just be a sampling of your gratitude, but what you write down becomes integrated more fully than what stays in the realm of unspoken thoughts. Let this page serve as a starting point and as one document of your gratitude.

➤ On each of the following cards, let your heart recall a special relative or loved one **who** is no longer living and **w**rite them a love note.

connecting to creativity and spirituality

Creativity and spirituality are two of our most potent connectors. When we're tapped in creatively, we say we're "in the flow" or "in the zone." When we're connected to something bigger than ourselves, which is the simplest definition of spirituality, we feel held and safe. As such, these energies—which are strands of the same braid—are some of our best anxiety reducers.

start and end your day with song

Singing is a Gold Star Practice, as it connects us to our hearts, bodies (singing releases endorphins and oxytocin), creativity/spirituality, ancestors (when we sing a song from our lineage), and others (when we sing in community).

Life is better with music. If you start your day with song—and especially if it's a song of gratitude from your lineage—you pave the pathway for joy. Many people are wired to default to anxiety first thing in the morning, which causes them to wake up feeling sluggish, anxious, and sometimes depressed. One way to counteract this tendency and rewire from disconnection to connection is to sing a song of gratitude, or any song that calls to you. This is the time to let go of the perfectionist or an idea you may have that you "can't sing." We're all singers; it's part of our birthright. This isn't about singing on pitch or beautifully. It's about connecting to your voice from the inside out.

This is also one way to set a healthy habit into motion, for one healthy action leads to the next. Once you start singing, you will likely find yourself humming, which activates the parasympathetic nervous system and sends a message to several spheres on the tree that all is well. Likewise, if you sing in the evening, you will likely find yourself humming your way into bedtime.

Write your morning song/chant here:

Write your evening song/chant here:

replace intrusive thoughts with a song

The creative sphere isn't only about what you create; it's also about opening to others' creative offerings and letting that fill you. Like finding a mantra that you can turn to during times of worry and to help break the rumination cycle, finding a song or two can help transmute the habit of negativity powered by the fuel source of fear to a soul-track of song run by goodness. We know how songs get stuck in our heads. I recommend singing your soul-song in the morning so this is what gets stuck in your head instead of intrusive thoughts. The brain has some need to be "stuck on repeat." Let's feed this need in a way that leads to more health and connection.

➔ **Use this space to write down the songs and song lyrics that make you feel most alive.**

Let this be creative. Write with markers or crayons, and open to any additional images that arise while you're transcribing the lyrics.

return to your dance

Dance is a Gold Star Practice, as it connects to the body, the soul, the heart, and spirituality. And when we dance in a group, we connect to others.

The impulse to move is as primal as the need to speak, and there are few people who don't love music and dance. I believe that, through dance, we can heal some of the wounds we carry about our bodies while also connecting to our natural creativity and the rhythm of the world. This isn't product-based creativity; it's the creativity that connects us to the flow of energy from our universe. We're not here to trademark or market any great moves that I'm sure will blossom in your kitchen! This is about creativity for the sake of connection, not production.

As children, we're naturally drawn to the rhythm of music, and our bodies naturally follow those rhythms. But when we dance as children, it's not long before self-consciousness overrides the natural joy and we develop inhibitions about dancing.

If you could shed the inhibitions and take the risk of being vulnerable, you would reclaim your joy for dancing. You would remember that dance helps you connect to the temple of your body, the pure and primal joy of being alive. It's not about image. It's not about being perfect or focusing on your perceived flaws. It's not about the outside body or how you look. It's about focusing your attention on the unchanging and intrinsic aspects of who you are: your heart, your breath, your passion, your feelings, your pain, your joy.

Dance! Dance with your partner or dance alone. Turn on your favorite music, play at least two songs to allow your body to settle in, close your eyes, dim the lights, and let your body follow its own rhythm, its own dance.

Don't look in the mirror. Just let yourself connect to the music and trust your body's response. This is about opening your heart and allowing whatever needs to happen, happen. If you want to cry, let yourself cry. If you want to scream, let yourself scream. The body stores our feelings and often when you open up these doors, old feelings rush to the surface. And sometimes, just sometimes, that feeling is joy and love. Let that in and out as well.

When you're done, take some notes about the experience. Invite imagery and color to be here as well. How did dancing feel?

connect to gratitude

"If the only prayer you ever say in your entire life is thank you, it will be enough."

—**Meister Eckhart**

If you're prone to anxiety, your mind has developed a habit of looking for what's wrong, hard, negative, or missing. One way to counteract that habit and create a new one that then helps you stay connected to the positive flow that weaves through our world is to practice gratitude throughout the day.

Sometimes we associate gratitude only with big-ticket items: health, family, financial security. These are wonderful things to be grateful for, but when we slow down, we can also narrow the aperture and focus on the micro-moments of gratitude:

Thank you for the beauty of sunlight on the trees.

Thank you for my warm bed.

Thank you for clean water.

No matter the circumstances of your life, you have an abundance of blessings for which you can be grateful. Perhaps you have all of your senses: you can see, hear, touch, feel, taste. Maybe you have all of your limbs: you can walk and write, dance and drive. Perhaps you have a safe and warm home and three meals a day. And you probably have at least one or two people in your life who support you and love you. These are blessings.

I am a big fan of a written and daily gratitude practice. I encourage you to open to the flow of blessings as they find you throughout the day, which means actively and consciously noticing when you experience well-being, beauty, awe, or gratitude. This could mean standing in the kitchen and realizing that you feel healthy and strong in your body; *thank you*. It could mean walking outside and noticing the puffy white clouds against a cerulean blue sky; *thank you*. It could mean looking at your child's face as they're falling asleep at night and allowing the infusion of love to well up inside of you; *thank you*.

Then write it down.

 Commit to seven days of writing down your gratitude and notice how you feel.

Let yourself be surprised by what arrives. Let it be different each day. Look for goodness throughout the day and write it down here. These pages will be a document of your gratitude and a testament to its power.

Day 1: _____

Day 2: _____

Day 3: _____

Day 4: _____

Day 5: _____

Day 6: _____

Day 7: _____

on repeat: from worry to mantra

We all get stuck in worry at times. We worry about our kids, our health, money, the planet. One of the most effective, on-the-spot tools for transforming worry into connection—which is another way of saying fear into trust—is to gather up the worry and place it on the wings of a mantra or a simple phrase that you repeat to connect with calm and strength.

Rumination is being stuck on repeat.

Mantra is intentional repeat.

One keeps us stuck.

One elevates us above the fear-fray and reconnects us to the web of flow and trust, the place of eternal song where we are held, connected, and safe.

Here are ideas for finding simple chants/mantras, and I encourage you to find your own. Search for "mantras for calm" or "mantras to reduce anxiety." You can include the word "secular" before your search if you'd like a nonreligious mantra, or you can include a word indicative of your culture, tradition, or religious practice.

→ **Make a list of any mantras that resonate with you and commit one to memory. The next time you notice that your mind is on worry-repeat, redirect to the mantra and repeat it several times.**

Some of my favorite mantras include:

- "All shall be well, and shall be well, and all manner of things shall be well." —Julian of Norwich

- "Thank you. I love you. I'm sorry. Please forgive me." —Ho'oponopono Hawaiian healing prayer

- "Hineini osah et atzmi merkavah L'Shechinah." —a Hebrew phrase that translates to "Here I am. Let me be a chariot for your will, Shechinah."

List your favorite mantras here, along with the tradition they're from:

bake bread

Baking bread is a Gold Star Practice that touches on multiple spheres: ancestral, body, friends and family, and creativity/spirituality. I'm placing it in the creative/spiritual sphere because this is often a vessel that connects to all other spheres, but it could also go in ancestors or body.

Baking bread is one of the oldest ways humans have related to food. Archaeological evidence shows that humans started baking bread 22,000 years ago. Wow! Every culture has its own ways of baking bread, and when we think back on our childhoods or conduct a bit of research, we will excavate those ways and memories.

The process of baking bread is rooting and connective. First, we decide on the recipe; I encourage you to find one from your tradition. Next, we pour and mix, then knead for several minutes, feeling our body strength as we connect with the dough. As you're kneading, put on some music from the tradition you're drawing from, and, if inspired, let yourself dance! Then the dough sits and rises, transforming from one state to another, just as we are constantly transitioning from one state of being to another.

Finally, we place the dough in the oven, where, again, it transforms and fills the house with the delicious and unmistakable smell of fresh bread.

When I make challah (traditional Jewish braided bread) with my sons on Fridays in preparation for Shabbat dinner, my whole body-mind-soul is transported to another time, and I can feel the week's anxiety dissolving away. I put on some Jewish music, and as I'm kneading the flour mixture, images of my foremothers come to me: I see my grandmother and aunts making their Jewish recipes in Los Angeles. I see my great-grandmother traversing the Atlantic when she was thirteen years old to live with two half brothers in New York, bravely forging a new life. Visions of my ancestors in the desert rise to mind as the bread rises throughout the day. These aren't necessarily literal visions—although they may be—as much as sense-memories that live in my cells and are called to life when I engage in rituals that link me through the generations.

 Baking bread can be intimidating, but I encourage you to give it a try!

Let this page become a document of your experience of baking bread.

Write or tape your recipe here:

Tape or glue a photograph of the finished bread here:

Reflect here on what arises, nourishes, and connects for you when you bake bread:

connecting to nature

many people turn to nature when they're needing connection, safety, clarity, and comfort. Nature can be a place to return to our essential nature and remember that we are held in an interconnected web of belonging. Held in the safety of this web, the unsafety that defines anxiety is absorbed.

Our experience with nature is enhanced when we develop an active, reciprocal relationship that is infused with conversation, curiosity, and gratitude. When we amplify our relationship with the natural world, we have a felt experience of well-being, and anxiety is pushed out to the edges.

be in nature

Everyone has access to nature to some degree. If you live in nature, it's easier to be in it, but even if you live in a city, you can always find some aspect of nature. Humans have messed up a lot when it comes to the natural world, but one of the things we've done right is create nature preserves, open spaces, and city parks. And nature herself insists on finding her way into the city; every city has trees, birds, insects, butterflies, bees, flowers, and grass to varying degrees. When we travel to New York City, I'm always amazed by how much nature lives in one of the most urban environments on the planet. From the birds outside of Grand Central Terminal to the masterpiece of Central Park, nature is accessible and alive.

Wherever you live, it requires effort to actually *be* in nature. We can look at the trees outside our windows, or we can go outside and sit next to the trees. I can appreciate the creek I can see from my studio, or I can make the effort to walk down the bank to sit with the creek. Being in nature is an entirely different experience from observing it.

→ To receive the infusion of nature's connective medicine, **we** must remove the pane of glass that separates us and **mak**e the effort to spend time in our local places of nature.

What are your nature spots?

_____
_____
_____
_____
_____

How do you feel when you make the effort to be in nature rather than simply observe it?

_____
_____
_____
_____
_____

The next time you're in nature, I invite you to respectfully gather a feather, stone, leaf, flower, pinecone, or any other element of nature and bring it into an indoor space as a way to remind yourself of your connection to nature. Sometimes just holding a leaf or stone can bring us back into that place of connection and encourage us to get back outside sooner rather than later.

befriend a tree

Growing up in Los Angeles, we had one spindly tree in the corner of our brick-clad backyard. I loved that little tree, and as I climbed her skinny branches, I imagined both of us in a vast forest of trees. I sat in her limbs and felt content. She was my friend and I was hers. We belonged to each other.

Children know that trees are friends. They know what many adults have forgotten: trees offer comfort, shade, beauty, fruit, and their gifts are amplified when we're in conscious connection with them. Connection requires spending time with a particular tree: sitting beneath it, touching it, and yes, even climbing it. When is the last time you climbed a tree?!

 Befriend a tree in your yard or neighborhood.

Make it a practice to spend time with this tree more days than not. Learn its name. Listen for its wisdom. Say hello to it every time you pass by, just as you would a good friend. It's such a small thing: to say hello to a tree, to thank it. But these small moments build up inside and create corridors of connection. As the tree begins to live in you, you remember that you belong to each other—that we are not separate—and anxiety is edged out.

↗ Create a mini shrine to your new friend on this page, a place to remember that she's close and accessible, even if you're not directly in her presence.

Draw your tree friend or take a photo of her and print it out, then tape it here. Bring back a fallen leaf or two and paste it onto this page. When you look at your tree friend, either here or wherever she stands, you can remember yourself back to the place of belonging. Notice the reduction of anxiety when you're in the felt-place of connection.

every stone tells a story

Like all connections, our connection with nature comes from the *relationship* we have with it. We know that nature offers peace, serenity, and a sense of well-being, but we tend to forget that we can deepen this sense of peace when we grow our relationship. This exercise asks that you suspend the disbelief that might come from your literalist, rationalist mind and dare to imagine that every element of nature, from the trees to the waters to the stones, has a story to tell.

 Go into nature and **find** a stone that calls to you.

Don't overthink it. Spend some time sitting with the stone and imagining what stories it has to tell. Who has it seen walking past? What other humans or animals have picked it up? How long has it been on the earth and how far back does its memory extend?

What wisdom might it have to share with you specifically about anxiety and worry?

_____
_____
_____
_____
_____
_____
_____
_____
_____
_____
_____
_____
_____

Keep the stone close by so when you see it, you remember its wisdom. When anxiety ramps up, hold the stone and ask for guidance. You might be surprised by the response you receive.

embraced by night

Nighttime, especially just before bed, is a liminal time when we feel more vulnerable and, thus, more prone to reach for our unhealthy coping strategies to manage anxiety. But if we can step out of our unhealthy habits, we can turn to the night as a source of wisdom and comfort. As Rabbi Zalman Schachter-Shalomi wrote:

> Every day we need to re-experience the moment in which we realize that we are integral to the universe, that we are part of it—not a separate entity only passing through. The Psalms tell us this: "You are my child. Today I have begotten you." When we re-experience this great awareness, we are regenerated. We need to reconnect with it every day, if only for a moment—it reestablishes our natural place in the order of the universe. When this connection happens, we are filled again with light, acceptance, and at-one-ment. For it to happen, we have to make time. Our ability to connect with the universe is especially strong at dawn and dusk, sunrise and sunset. Whenever you can, spend that time waking your soul. This is how you can strengthen your connection with organic time.

Take a moment before you get into bed, after you turn off the screens, to slow down into organic time.

Let yourself be led to an open window. Breathe in the cool night air. Listen to the sounds. There may be traffic sounds, yes, but see if you can listen beneath the traffic to the sounds of night. Look up to the sky. No matter where you are, no matter if you live in the country or a city, a patch of sky is always available to you. Breathe it in.

Look for stars.

Notice the phase of the moon.

Allow your face to be kissed by night.

No books, no screens, no words silent or spoken.

Walk to the window and breathe in only stars, the Seven Sisters constellation, seen or veiled, that guide you into sleep the way they led sailors into new lands long ago.

Seek direction from the quiet spaces inside, the wisdom encoded in the trees.

Write down what you notice. If there's a particular constellation that calls you, do some research and write about it here. Draw the constellation. Note any moon wisdom or tree comfort. Trust it and write about it.

conclusion

There are infinitely more ways to connect than what I've shared in this workbook. My hope is that, by exploring the pathways of connection that I've presented here, you will open to other avenues that are already present in your life or that you would like to explore. In reality, the Tree of Life image that I've shared has many more branches extending from both sides, and branches extending from those branches. Connectivity is infinite; it's only our human minds that can become trapped in the small idea that there are only a few ways to connect.

At the same time, what I've shared is enough. If you engage with even just a couple of practices in each section, you will notice a reduction in your anxiety levels. And the more you practice, the more you replace the pervasive sense of unsafety that defines anxiety with the expansive sense of safety that arises from connection. The work works exponentially and nonlinearly; one practice opens portals and pathways that dovetail with another practice, and you start to notice that you're feeling more connected than you were the day before. Inner work doesn't proceed in a straight line. Rather, it occurs in layers and spirals. We connect and we disconnect. Our hearts open and close. We inhale and exhale. We have a sense of belonging and also a sense of isolation. We remember and we forget. As such, please be kind to yourself as you practice the art of connection as a way to calm anxiety.

If you find yourself disconnecting and forgetting, I encourage you to pull out this workbook and read through its pages. As I mentioned in the introduction, this is meant to be a keepsake book—not in the sense that it's overly precious, but in the sense that it can keep the sense-memory close of what it feels like to be in connection. Sometimes just looking at an image that you drew or a photograph that you glued into the book can transport you across what feels like a vast divide of isolation into the heart of the forest, where all beings are connected to you and you are connected to all beings.

Connection is closer than you think. It's in your heart, your mind, your body, your soul. It's in your relationships, your community, your purpose. It's with the ancestors, in your creativity, in nature.

It's in your hands, right now, in this book, just a breath away. Sometimes, when I finish a book I've loved, I start it over again immediately. If that has been your experience with this book—and I hope that it has!—I invite you to start over. Go back to the beginning. Read through the pages that stood out for you. And know that I am with you as a guide and a source of connection. Through these words, we are connected to each other, and you are connected to every other person who is carrying this book in their heart or keeps it on their bedside table. Sometimes even just that simple thought is enough to remind us that, no matter how it seems, we are never, ever alone. Now, back to page 1.

acknowledgments

As gratitude is the connective stream that flows through every hour of my life, it brings me great joy to express gratitude here. I've loved writing every word of this book, but this might be my favorite part.

I'm deeply grateful to Sarah Stanton at Sounds True for approaching me with the invitation to write this book. I'm humbled and honored by your belief in me, and deeply grateful to be in creative collaboration with Sounds True again.

To my clients, blog readers, podcast listeners, and course members: thank you for allowing me to walk alongside you as you repair attachment wounds and learn to trust. You are all treasures.

To the trees, stones, water, grasses, bees, and animals with whom we share this land: *thank you*. You are among my greatest teachers, and my daily and nightly relationships with you informed the essence of this book.

Thank you to my ancestors who guided and loved me when you were here and continue to surround me with comfort and wisdom from another realm. Grandma Charlotte and Grandpa Izzy, Aunt Esther, Aunt Anne, Aunt Bea, Great-Grandma Sarah: *thank you*.

To my cousins Leslie Kendall Dye and Jennifer Engelberg Bader, and to my aunt Marilyn Zweifach: our reconnection at this stage of life is a gift beyond words.

I wasn't blessed with blood sisters in this lifetime, but I've been blessed with soul sister-friends. Jessica Hicks, Carrie Dinow, Lisa Rappaport: you are my deepest sources of female connection. Sandra Snyder and Jennifer Hirschorn: our monthly moon group and our friendship sustain me more than you know.

Victoria Russell, my niece, podcast cohost, and dear friend: I'm grateful every day for your presence in my life. Our *Gathering Gold* podcast has changed my work life in ways I could have never dreamed when we started it in the spring of 2021. It weaves like a gold thread throughout this workbook.

Instagram is a ride, but I'm deeply grateful that it brought me two amazing women who have become both colleagues and cherished friends: Megan deBoer and Silvy Khoucasian.

Thank you to my two incredible sons, Everest and Asher, who teach me about healthy attachment, including the art of letting go, every day.

Finally, to my husband, Daev Finn, my forever soulmate, my partner in every sense of the word, my biggest fan, my root and crown, my light, my teacher: thank you for buying all my chairs.

recommended resources

The Wisdom of Anxiety: How Worry and Intrusive Thoughts Are Gifts to Help You Heal, by Sheryl Paul

- Offers a more in-depth exploration of the four realms of self

Break Free from Anxiety: A Nine-Month Course on the Art of Living—conscious-transitions.com/courses

- An in-depth course to help you heal anxiety at the root, which includes personal guidance and regular group meetings

about the author

Sheryl Lisa Finn has guided thousands of people worldwide through the tricky terrain of anxiety through her courses, blog, books, and private sessions. She became intimately familiar with anxiety when she had her first panic attack at age twenty-one, and since then, she has been devoted to studying the terrain of the inner world. Sheryl received her master's degree in counseling from Pacifica Graduate Institute, specializing in Jungian depth psychology.

Sheryl is the author of three books—*The Conscious Bride*, *The Conscious Bride's Wedding Planner*, and *The Wisdom of Anxiety*—and she has been featured on the *Oprah Winfrey Show*, *Good Morning America*, and other media. She writes a weekly blog and cohosts the *Gathering Gold* podcast with her niece, Victoria Russell. Sheryl lives in Colorado with her husband, and together they've raised two wonderful sons. Learn more about Sheryl and her work through her blog and website at conscious-transitions.com.

about sounds true

Sounds True was founded in 1985 by Tami Simon with a clear mission: to disseminate spiritual wisdom. Since starting out as a project with one woman and her tape recorder, we have grown into a multimedia publishing company with a catalog of more than 3,000 titles by some of the leading teachers and visionaries of our time, and an ever-expanding family of beloved customers from across the world.

In more than three decades of evolution, Sounds True has maintained our focus on our overriding purpose and mission: to wake up the world. We offer books, audio programs, online learning experiences, and in-person events to support your personal growth and awakening, and to unlock our greatest human capacities to love and serve.

At SoundsTrue.com you'll find a wealth of resources to enrich your journey, including our weekly *Insights at the Edge* podcast, free downloads, and information about our nonprofit Sounds True Foundation, where we strive to remove financial barriers to the materials we publish through scholarships and donations worldwide.

To learn more, please visit SoundsTrue.com/freegifts or call us toll-free at 800.333.9185.

Together, we can wake up the world.

sounds true inner workbooks

Accessible, self-paced, and deeply transformative workbooks, guided by some of the most trusted voices in psychology and spirituality.

Also by Sheryl Lisa Finn

The Wisdom of Anxiety: How Worry and Intrusive Thoughts Are Gifts to Help You Heal (as Sheryl Paul)

The Conscious Bride: Women Reveal Their True Feelings about Getting Hitched (as Sheryl Paul)

The Conscious Bride's Wedding Planner: How to Prepare Emotionally, Practically, and Spiritually for a Meaningful and Joyous Wedding (as Sheryl Paul)

the healing anxiety workbook

expertise, it's a must-have resource for anyone committed to understanding and moving through anxiety."

Dr. Lauren Fogel Mersy
coauthor of *Desire*

"In a world of growing disconnection and anxiety, Sheryl Lisa Finn provides ideas for reconnecting with oneself, family, society, and nature. Her book offers something new in the world of anxiety workbooks. Finn's approach is practical while also respecting the deeper aspects of ourselves and the larger world we inhabit."

Stuart Ralph
psychotherapist and host of *The OCD Stories* podcast

"What a gift! Opening Sheryl Lisa Finn's exquisite new book, I immediately felt seen, loved, challenged, and comforted all at once. At its center stands the transcultural Tree of Life, whose compassionate presence grounds a vulnerable, authentic (and joyful!) exploration of Self, Others, and the Unseen. Through Finn's beautiful inquiries and exercises, we learn to shelter in the roots and branches of our own wise self—the source of true and lasting calm."

Lyanda Lynn Haupt
author of *Rooted*

Praise for *The Healing Anxiety Workbook*

"*The Healing Anxiety Workbook* is an exceptional guide for anyone struggling with anxiety. Its thoughtful exercises and compassionate insights make it more than just a workbook—it's a true companion on the path to healing. The emphasis on connection, both with oneself and others, creates a powerful foundation for lasting change. This workbook doesn't just offer symptom relief—it encourages deep, transformative growth. I highly recommend it to anyone ready to move beyond anxiety and embrace a life of inner peace and connection."

Barry McDonagh
author of *DARE*

"*The Healing Anxiety Workbook* is a masterful blend of soulful wisdom, playfulness, and the soothing essence of mother nature. It offers not only a variety of practical support but also heartfelt insights for anyone navigating their anxiety journey. This workbook serves as a beacon of hope and comfort, providing readers with the tools and encouragement to find peace, joy, and resilience every step of the way."

Silvy Khoucasian
relationship coach

"If you're looking for a compassionate guide to navigating anxiety, *The Healing Anxiety Workbook* by Sheryl Lisa Finn is an essential read. With her gentle approach, Finn offers readers actionable strategies to gain a greater sense of peace and connection. Included is a treasure trove of tools, wisdom, and companionship on the journey to emotional well-being. With its blend of empathy and

Printed in Great Britain
by Amazon